MW01199421

An Introduction to Karaite Judaism:
History, Theology, Practice, and Custom

A Publication of the al-Qirqisani Center
for the Promotion of Karaite Studies

An Introduction to Karaite Judaism: History, Theology, Practice, and Custom. Copyright © 2003 Karaism.com and the al-Qirqisani Center for the Promotion of Karaite Studies. All rights reserved. Printed in the United States of America. No portion of this book may be reprinted, reproduced or used in any manner except that implied by sale, and in the case of brief citations for the purpose of critical articles and reviews. For information send inquiries to the al-Qirqisani Center for the Promotion of Karaite Studies 164 9th Street, Troy, NY 12180-2910, or books-@karaitejudaism.com

Library of Congress Card Number: 2001117259

ISBN 0-9700775-4-8 (hdbk.)

An Introduction to Karaite Judaism:
History, Theology, Practice, and Custom

THE SPECIAL OCCASIONS OF LIFE

Table of Names

'Amos [Amos]
'Ezra' [Ezra]
'Ovadyah [Obadiah]
Avraham [Abraham]
Avram [Abram]
BeMidbar [Numbers]
Bere'shit [Genesis]
Dani'el [Daniel]
Devarim [Deuteronomy]
Eikhah [Lamentations]
Ester [Esther]
Haggai [Haggai]
Havaqquq [Habakkuk]
Hoshe'a' [Hosea]
Iyyov [Job]
Mal'akhi [Malachi]
Mikhah [Micah]
Mishlei [Proverbs]
Mosheh [Moses]
Nahum [Nahum]
Nehemyah [Nehemiah]
Qohelet [Ecclesiastes]
Rut [Ruth]
Sefanyah [Zephaniah]
Shaul [Saul]

Shemot [Exodus]
Shemu'el Alef [1 Samuel]
Shemu'el Beit [I and II Samuel]
Shir HaShirim [Song of Songs]
Shofetim [Judges]
Tehillim [Psalms]
Wayyiqra' [Leviticus]
Ya'aqov [Jacob]
Yehezq'el [Ezekiel]
Yehoshu'a' [Joshua]
Yerushalayim [Jerusalem]
Yesha'yahu [Isaiah]
Yirmiyahu [Jeremiah]
Yishaq [Isaac]
Yisra'el [Israel]
Yo'el [Joel]
Yonah [Jonah]
Zekharyah [Zechariah]

Introduction

Writing a volume on the beliefs and practices of Karaite Judaism may, to some, seem strange. After all, one of the fundamental tenants of Karaite Judaism is that the *TaNaKh*, the Jewish scriptures, is the sole source of Jewish law, and the final authority on theological and legal issues. What the Torah does not provide is interpretation and explanation. Ostensibly, this is the reason behind the Talmud. And, conceptually, there is nothing wrong with a Talmud. Karaites have always maintained this. Several prominent figures in Karaite Judaism have written scholarly works on Biblical interpretation, and legal explanation, which is what the Talmud claims to be. Furthermore, one finds examples of Biblical interpretation in the *TaNaKh* itself. For example, in the book of Nehemyah 8.14-15 it is written:

> And they found written in the Torah, which יהוה commanded through Mosheh, that the Children of Yisra'el should dwell in arbor-booths during the pilgrimage festival of the seventh month, and that they should announce and proclaim in all their cities and in Yerushalayim, saying, "Go out to the mountain, and bring olive branches, branches of oil trees, myrtle branches, date palm branches, and branches of densely leafed trees, to make arbor booths, as [it is] written".

This is an interpretation of Wayyiqra' 23.40:

> And you shall take for yourselves by the first day the produce of splendorous trees: branches of date palm trees, the boughs of densely leafed trees, and willows of the brook; and you shall rejoice before יהוה your God for seven days.

The Karaite objection to the Talmud lies in the fact that the Rabbanites contend the Talmud is more important, and more authoritative than the Torah. For them, it replaces the Torah. The *Talmud Bavli, Masekhet Berakhot* 28b says:

> "Restrain your sons from Hegayon [reading the text (of the TaNaKh)], and seat them between the knees of the Rabbis".

Rashi, in his commentary on the Talmud Bavli, explains this:

> "From Hegayon: Do not train (or accustom) them too much in (the reading of) Miqra' [the text of the TaNaKh]".

Moreover, though it claimed the Torah as its source, the Talmud contradicted the Torah; it added to and took away from the Torah, and brought into Judaism many unwelcome pagan elements.[1]

Aside from these fundamental issues of faith, Rabbanism and Karaism differ on basic issues of philosophy and methodology. For example, a central tenet of Rabbanism is the veneration of custom. Custom is, perhaps, the defining element of Rabbanism. In many cases in the Rabbanite legal system, a custom will override a law. For example, *Maskhet Soferim, Pereq 14, Mishnah* 20 says:

> "*Halakhah* is not decided until it becomes custom, as it is said custom overrides *Halakhah*"

This is not the case in Karaite Judaism, where a logically sound, valid interpretation of the Biblical text will always override a custom. In sum, we see one of the main differences between the two systems lies in their philosophical and methodological foundations. Rabbanism is founded on custom and

---

1 See Zvi Cahn's, "The Rise of The Karaite Sect".

precedent, while Karaism is founded on interpretation and reason.[2]

All of this being said, it must be noted that, generally, the Torah does not need to be explained. Its meaning may most easily be derived from a plain, simple reading of the Biblical text. What requires explanation, from a legal perspective, are the many elements of modernity that the Torah was unaware of, but that directly relate to its prescriptions and prohibitions – and the elements of the ancient world that we have lost touch with. For example, is one permitted to use electric lights on the Sabbath? What are the implications of processing on the purity (*tum'ah* and *tahorah*) status of processed foods? How are we to understand what the Torah meant when it forbade images? For example, are we allowed to own pieces of art? These issues, and many others, very logically and directly relate back to Torah law, but their relationship may not be readily apparent to the modern individual.

It is with this intent – to address the issues of modernity, and provide for the preservation of valuable custom – that this volume was prepared.

A Note on formatting in this volume: The reader may notice that certain words are consistently italicized in this volume. The reason for this is to differentiate English from non-English words. All non-English words have been italicized, except for the names of the books of the *TaNaKh* and the names of places and persons. Finally, Rather than using the word God, or HaShem, or YHWH, out of respect, we always print God's name, where it occurs, as: יהוה

---

2 A modern analogy can be found that parallels this in the differences between the French and English/American legal systems – the French resembling the Karaite system, and the English the Rabbanite.

Foundations

CHAPTER 1

The Roots of our Faith

The Covenant And The People

The essence of our nation, the foundation of our people may be found in the covenants made between our ancestors and יהוה. It is these covenants that founded the Jewish people, and gave us a special relationship to יהוה. It is these covenants that created and maintain the Jewish religion. It is these covenants that define who is and who may become a part of the Jewish nation.

The first covenant יהוה made with the Jewish people was with the father of the Jewish people, Avraham (also known as Avram):

> Bere'shit 17.1-8
> And, when Avram was ninety-nine years old, יהוה appeared to Avram and said to him, "I am El Shaddai. Walk before me and be whole-hearted. I will establish My covenant between Me and you, and I will make you exceedingly numerous". Avram fell upon his face; and יהוה spoke to him saying, "Behold this is My covenant with you: You shall be the father of a multitude of nations. And your name shall no longer be called Avram, but your name shall be Avraham, for I make you the father of a multitude of nations. I will make you exceedingly fertile, and make nations of you; and kings

1

shall come forth from you. I will maintain My covenant between Me and you, and your offspring after you throughout their generations, as an eternal covenant, to be God to you and to your offspring after you. I will give the land of your sojourning to you and your offspring after you, all the land of Cana'an, as an eternal holding. I will be God to them".

This is an everlasting covenant, the fulfilment of which is realized every time a Jewish community celebrates the *Berit Milah* [circumcision ceremony]. It was passed on from father to son, mother to daughter. We see, in fact, that when the people of Yisra'el entered into their covenant with יהוה as a nation, their covenant with יהוה as a family (the covenant with Avraham) remained intact. As indicated above, all members of the nation of Yisra'el are still required to circumcise their sons; and the promise of the Land of Yisra'el has remained a part of our heritage.

This is a covenant that is marked in the flesh (for males) by circumcision. Such an indelible mark as circumcision creates an ever-present reminder, and an inescapable association with the people of יהוה. Any man who is a member of the Jewish people, or any man who would become a member of the Jewish people, must be circumcised:

Bere'shit 17.11
You shall circumcise the flesh of your foreskin, and it shall be the sign of the covenant between Me and you.

Bere'shit 17.14
"...And an uncircumcised male who does not circumcise the flesh of his foreskin, that person shall be cut off from his people; he has broken My covenant".

From the time of Avraham, through the en-
slavement in Egypt, the Jewish people were a family. We are a
family to this day, and as such, we have always maintained a
sense of family. We are a large, diverse, far-flung family, but a
family nevertheless. Membership in the family has been determined by birth, but never restricted by it. A child born to a
Jewish father is considered Jewish by birth. Converts, those who
wish to join the Jewish nation (naturalize), have always been and
continue to be welcome. Given that we are a family, those who
wish to join the Jewish people are more than converts to a
religion or naturalized citizens; they are adopted into the family
of Avraham.

It was this covenant with Avraham, inherited by his sons
Yishaq and Ya'aqov, and their physical and spiritual descendants, that יהוה remembered when he came to free the Yisra'el
ites from slavery in Egypt, to make them a nation:

Shemot 6.2-8
And יהוה spoke to Moses and said to him, "I am יהוה.
I appeared to Avraham, to Yishaq, and to Ya'aqov
as El Shaddai, but I did not make Myself known to
them by My name יהוה. I also established My covenant with them, to give them the land of Cana'an,
the land of their sojournings in which they lived as
sojourners. Now I have heard the moaning of the
Yisra'el ites whom the Egyptians are enslaving,
and I have remembered My covenant. Say, therefore, to the Yisra'el ite people: I am יהוה, and I will
bring you out from under the burden of Egypt, and
deliver you from their bondage, and I will redeem
you with an outstretched arm and through great
acts of judgment And I will take you to be My people, and I will be God to you, and you shall know
that I am יהוה, your God, who brought you out from
under the burdens of Egypt. And I will bring you
into the land which I raised My hand [in an oath]

to give to Avraham, to Yishaq, and to Ya'aqov, and I will give it to you for an inheritance, I יהוה".

Our covenant with יהוה gives us a special relationship to Him, enjoyed by no other people. We are יהוה's treasure. יהוה has taken special care to watch over us. He personally saw to our redemption from Egypt; and he continues to watch over us to this day.

> Devarim 4.32-34
> For inquire now about bygone ages that came before you, from the day when יהוה created man on earth, and from one end of heaven to the other, has anything as grand as this ever happened, or has its like ever been heard of? Has any people heard the voice of a god speaking from the midst of fire, as you have, and lived? Or has any god ventured to go and take for himself one nation from the midst of another by provings, by signs and portents, by war, by a mighty hand and an outstretched arm and awe-inspiring deeds, as all that יהוה your God did for you in Egypt before your eyes?

Moreover, יהוה has entrusted us with great responsibilities. We are more than just a nation, we are also יהוה's trusted partner, His priesthood.

> Shemot 19.4-8
> "'You have seen what I did to Egypt, how I bore you on vultures' wings and brought you to Me. Now then, if you will hearken to My voice and keep My covenant, you shall be a treasured possession to Me from among all peoples, for all the earth is Mine. And you shall be to Me a kingdom of priests and a holy nation.' These are the words that you shall speak to the children of Yisra'el ". And

Mosheh came and summoned the elders of the people and put before them all that יהוה had commanded. And all the people answered together and said, "All that יהוה has spoken we will do!" And Mosheh brought back the people's words to יהוה.

The Exodus grew out of a covenant, the covenant with Avraham, and led to a covenant, the covenant at Sinai. Throughout our history, our greatest moments have been those where we have encountered יהוה in covenant. In fact, we look forward to the time when we will meet יהוה again in covenant (Yirmiyahu 31.31). Our covenants with יהוה stand out as the most significant aspects of our Jewishness, and bind us – family, nation, and religion – together.

The Land Of Yisra'el

Devarim 34.4
And יהוה said to him (Mosheh): "this is the land which I swore to Avraham, to Yishaq, and to Ya'aqov, 'I will give it to your children.'"

There is an inseparable bond that exists between the people of Yisra'el and the land of Yisra'el. Perhaps no other people in the history of the world have been so attached to a specific land. The land of Yisra'el has been a part of the longing of the people of Yisra'el since before the nation of Yisra'el existed. The land of Yisra'el is our promise and heritage; it is a part of our redemption; and it is our responsibility. It is an integral part of our religion; and it is a part of our Jewish soul.

The Torah is replete with references to the promise יהוה made to Avraham that his descendants would inherit the land of Yisra'el . As soon as Avraham appears in the Torah, the land is mentioned (Bere'shit 12.1); and the promise of land, though not specifically stated, hangs as an unspoken expectation waiting to be fulfilled. From that time forward, the land is mentioned fourteen times in connection with יהוה's promise to give it to the descendants of Avraham in the book of Bere'shit alone.

Throughout our history, this promise has been preserved from generation to generation, passed down through familial lines. Even after our ancestors possessed the land, the promise still played a prominent rôle in the consciousness of Yisra'el, as can be seen from the following passages from the *TaNaKh* that were written when Yisra'el was a nation.

> Shofetim 2.1
> An angel of יהוה came up from Gilgal to Bokhim and said, "I brought you up from Egypt and I took you into the land which I had promised on oath to your fathers. And I said, 'I will never break My covenant with you.'"

> Shemu'el Alef 12.6
> Shemu'el [Samuel] said to the people, "יהוה [is witness], He who appointed Mosheh and Aharon [Aaron] and who brought your fathers out of the land of Egypt.

> Nehemyah 9.23
> You made their children as numerous as the stars of heaven, and brought them to the land which You told their fathers to go and possess.

> Yehezq'el 47.14
> ...and you shall share the rest equally. As I swore to give it to your fathers, so shall this land fall to you as your heritage.

Our promise of the land is not a promise of ownership. The land is יהוה's. Our promise from יהוה is that we will be able to take care of the land. In order to preserve this promise, we must live up to the terms of our covenant with יהוה. We are told that the reason the Cana'anites were torn from the land stemmed from their defilement of it, which was rooted in their evil practices.

> Wayyiqra' 18.24-28
> Do not defile yourselves with any of these things; for by all these the nations are defiled, which I am casting out before you. You shall therefore keep My statutes and My judgments, and shall not commit [any] of these abominations, any of your own nation or any resident alien who dwells among you. For the land is defiled; therefore I visit the punishment of its iniquity upon it, and the land vomits out its inhabitants. (for all these abominations the men of the land have done, who [were] before you, and thus the land is defiled), lest the land vomit you out also when you defile it, as it vomited out the nations that [were] before you.

This is one of the main reasons why the promise of land has remained such an important part of the religious thought of the Jews through the ages. Consequently, we are told, through the commandments that relate to the land, how to keep it from defilement.

> BeMidbar 35.33
> So you shall not pollute the land where you [are;] for blood defiles the land, and no atonement can be made for the land, for the blood that is shed on it, except by the blood of him who shed it.

> Devarim 21.23
> His corpse shall not remain on the tree overnight, for must bury him that [same] day because a hanged man is a reproach to יהוה and you shall not defile your land that יהוה your God is giving you for a possession.

Devarim 24.4
[He may not take her to] wife ... she has been defiled;
for that [is] an abomination before יהוה, and you shall
not bring sin on the land which יהוה your God is giving
you [as] an inheritance.

Our responsibility goes beyond simply keeping the land
from defilement by remaining holy. We are also charged with
caring for the land. In the mind of the Torah, the land is a living
entity; it is not just dirt. It must rest. It must be tended. It must
be protected.

Wayyiqra' 26.34
Then shall the land be paid her Sabbath years all
the days of the desolation when you are in the land
of your enemies; then shall the land rest and be
paid her its Sabbath years.

BeMidbar 35.30-34
Whoever kills a person, the murderer shall be put
to death on the testimony of witnesses; but one
witness is not [sufficient] testimony against a person for the death [penalty] 'Moreover you shall take
no ransom for the life of a murderer who [is] guilty
of death, but he shall surely be put to death... 'So
you shall not pollute the land where you [are;] for
blood defiles the land, and no atonement can be
made for the land, for the blood that is shed on it,
except by the blood of him who shed it. 'Therefore
do not defile the land which you inhabit, in the
midst of which I dwell; for I יהוה dwell among the
children of Yisra'el .' "

The land is holy. What does this mean? One way of understanding this is to look at what it means to be an 'am qadosh,
a holy people. The people of Yisra'el are holy, in part because we
are supposed to be an example to the rest of the world. Our

attachment to our land, and our care for it is one of the ways we are supposed to create that example. One of the ways in which the land derives its holiness is from the fact that the world will watch how we treat it, and take note. They will emulate how the people of יהוה take care of their land, and that will impact how the rest of the earth is cared for.

The most brilliant drama surrounding our possession of the land of Yisra'el is the story of our Exodus from Egypt. The Exodus is the spark of our beginning as a nation and our redemption as a people. It is the fire from which we were moulded and out of which the words of the Torah came to life. The ultimate end of the Exodus, its culmination, is our possession of the land of Yisra'el.

> Shemot 3.8
> So I have come down to deliver them out of the hand of the Egyptians, and to bring them up from that land to a good and large land, to a land flowing with milk and honey, to the place of the Cana'anites and the Hittites and the Amorites and the Perizzites and the Hivites and the Jebusites...

Karaites have, perhaps, been more pronounced than others in their connection with the land. Many prominent Karaite leaders have contended that we are commanded to live in the land of Yisra'el . Dani'el al-Qumisi, writing at the end of the ninth century wrote:

> Know, then, that the scoundrels who are among Yisra'el say, one to another, "It is not our duty to go to Yerushalayim until He shall gather us together, just as it was He who had cast us abroad". These are the words of those who would draw the wrath of יהוה and who are bereft of sense... Therefore it is incumbent upon you who are in awe of יהוה to come to Yerushalayim and to dwell in it, in

order to hold vigils before יהוה until the day when Yerushalayim is restored.

The land, is not only an important part of our history and heritage, it is also an important part of our soul. The land of Yisra'el is of such significance in Jewish life that it transcends the bounds of religious and non-religious Jews. Even if we have not been able to unite as a people on our understanding of the covenant, the central defining point of who we are, we have been able to come together on our feelings about the land of Yisra'el. This is can be seen quite dramatically in Yisra'el 's centuries long messianic passion:

> Yesha'yahu 35.10
> And the ransomed of יהוה shall return and come with exultation to Siyyon [Zion] and eternal joy upon their heads. They shall attain joy and glad-ness, and sorrow and sighing shall flee.

> Zekharyah 10.9-10
> I sowed them among the nations and in the distant places they shall remember Me, and they shall live, along with their children, and shall return. I will bring them back from the land of Egypt and gather them from Assyria; and I will bring them to the land of Gil'ad [Gilead] and Lebanon, and [even] they (the land of Gil'ad [Gilead] and Lebanon) shall not be sufficient for them.

However, it is perhaps the Psalmist, who sums up best the feeling we have had over the centuries for our God-given land:

> Tehillim 137.5-6
> If I forget you, O Yerushalayim, let my right hand wither; let my tongue stick to my palate if I do not

remember you, if I do not elevate Yerushalayim above my chiefest joy.

The God Of Yisra'el

The God of Yisra'el is unlike any other deity in history. The very thought of His existence challenged all the notions of godhood and the nature of the relationship between God and man that existed when the Torah was written. Standing out to this day in sharp contrast to the religions of the world is the singular, compassionate God of Yisra'el who is in complete control of the creation with which He so lovingly endowed all mankind, His proudest achievement.

It is our faith in one God, יהוה alone, that has most significantly separated us out from among the nations. Perhaps the most famous passage in all of the scriptures is Devarim 6.4.

Devarim 6.4
Hear, O Yisra'el ! יהוה is our God, יהוה is one.

In a Western world dominated by Islam and Christianity, it is often difficult to relate back to an age when the common mind was dominated by a pantheon of raging deities which had to be calmed and placated – deities who were capricious, politically or sexually motivated, and untrustworthy. This, however, was the world stage upon which the children of Yisra'el entered with their dissonant assertion that one God ruled and empowered creation.

Yesha'yahu 40.12-14
Who measured the waters with the hollow of His hand, and meted out the skies with a span,
And comprehended the dust of the earth in a shalish-measure [one third of an 'efah],
And weighed the mountains with a balance and the hills with a scale?

Who has measured the spirit of יהוה, and what man could tell Him His plan?
Whom did He consult, and who taught Him, and guided Him in the way of judgment?
And guided Him in knowledge and showed Him the path of wisdom?

Eliyahu Bashyachi, Aderet Eliyahu on the ten principles of faith:
All physical creation, i.e., the planets and all that is upon them, has been created. It has been created by a Creator who did not create Himself, but is eternal. The Creator has no likeness and is unique in all respects.

Yefet Ben-'Eli HaLewi, Commentary on Ruth, 1.1
Blessed be the God of Yisra'el , the Primeval and Most Glorious, who created everything for the revelation of His omnipotence, and made the heavens the seat of the throne of His supreme dignity...

More than this, more than the fact that there was one God, יהוה was just. He was not fickle and easily angered. He was not subject to whims and fancies, but held a deep, heart-felt concern for the creation that was the work of his hands. He was intimately concerned about our welfare and how we treat each other.

BeMidbar 23.19
יהוה is not man and that He should deceive, or a human that He should change His mind.
Would He have said and not act, and have spoken and not carry it out?

Shemot 22.21
You shall not afflict any widow or orphan.

Shemot 23.9
And you shall not oppress a resident alien, you know the soul of the resident alien for having yourselves been resident aliens in the land of Egypt.

Aharon Ben-Eliyahu, 'Es Hayyim Chapter 79
...we must explain that He [יהוה] governs and sets in order everything that exists in a good and perfect order – righteously and without perversion – and that only good may be found in Him, as attested to by Moses in his statement, "And יהוה saw everything that He had made, and behold it was very good", and the words of the Psalmist, "יהוה is good to all".

The pagan deities were thought to be controllable by means of knowing their name, or participating in rituals that made things on heaven as they were on earth. The Ba'al Shem, or master of the Name, in the Rabbanite tradition is one who can work miracles because he knows how to use one of יהוה's names. The Christians, believe they can work miracles, through the power of the name "Jesus". The God of Yisra'el , however, has made it very clear that He can not be controlled or manipulated, by use of his name or any other means. He is fully in charge.

Shemot 3.13-15
And Moses said to יהוה, "When I come to the Yisra'el ites and say to them 'The God of your fathers has sent me to you,' and they ask me, 'What is His name?' what shall I say to them?" And יהוה said to Moses, "Ehyeh-Asher-Ehyeh"[I am/will be that which I am/will be]. He continued, "Thus shall you say to the Yisra'el ites, 'Ehyeh [I am/will be] sent me to you.'" And יהוה said further to Moses, "Thus shall you speak to the Yisra'el ites: יהוה [He is/will be], the God of your fathers, the God of

Avraham, the God of Yishaq, and the God of Ya'aqov, has sent me to you: This shall be My name forever and this My appellation throughout all generations.

Aharon Ben-Eliyahu, 'Es Hayyim, Chapter 74:
When Moses states, "When I come to the Yisra'el ites... and they ask me, "What is His name?" what shall I say to them? He is referring to the second signification by which יהוה was not known to the patriarchs. The verse means – they will say to me: By virtue of what power have you come to deliver us from Egypt ?

Martin Buber, a Selection from "Kingship of God"
Moses then resists somewhat, and asks the being speaking to him from the Burning Bush, the being sending him on this extraordinary mission to Egypt, "Here, I will come to the Children of Yisra'el /and I will say to them:

> *The God of your fathers has sent me to you,*
> *and they will say to me: What is his name? –*
> *and what shall I say to them then?" (Shemot 3.13).*

Scholars have rightly posited that the question, "What is his name" has to do with primitive beliefs concerning names. It was then a common conviction that through a knowledge of a god's name one could have the god himself in one's power; but we must also add that these beliefs were stronger among the Egyptians than among any other ancient people... Moses is not assuming that his people will, when he says he is sent by the God of their fathers, then ask: "So, what is his name?" Such nonsense would be incomprehensible in any people, let alone in this people, whose conscious-

ness of its own tradition the author of the Burning
Bush episode is surely not calling into question...
The question Moses expects from his people concerns not the letter of the name, but its secret, its
particular articulation, its magic use. The afflicted
will, Moses thinks, want to know (in accord with
what they see in Egypt) how they can invoke יהוה
with power, so that he will appear at once to them
and help them. יהוה's message will not be enough
for them; they will want, rather, to possess him...
And יהוה answers him with his ehyeh asher ehyeh...
The word does not mean "I am who I am" or anything similar, since hayah, hawah in biblical language means "is" only (and only secondarily) in a
copulative sense, and never in an existential one...
Ehyeh in our passage means precisely what it
means in the same story both before (3.12) and
after (4.12 and 15): to be present to someone, to be
with someone, to assist someone – except that here
the verb is used absolutely, without any specifica-
tion of whom the one-who-is-there is for. יהוה does
not by this make any theological proposition that
he is eternal or self-sufficient; rather he offers to
the creature he has made, to his person and his
people, the assurance that they are in need of and
that renders all magical feats both void and super-
fluous. The first ehyeh says simply, "I shall be
there" (with my host, with my people, with you) –
so you do not need to conjure me up; and the next
asher ehyeh can according to all parallel passages
(as in Exodus 16.23, 33.19) mean only "as the one
I shall always be there as", "as who I shall on this
or that occasion be-there as", i.e., just as I shall on
this or that occasion want to appear. I myself, יהוה
says, do not anticipate my own manifestations –
and yet you think by some means or other to con-
strain me to appear here and not elsewhere, now

and not elsewhere, so and not otherwise! Or, in summary, you do not need to invoke me; but neither are you able to invoke me. What is here reported is, in the context of the history of religion, the demagicalizing of belief – in the self-proclamation of the God present to his own, abiding with his own, accompanying his own.

In contrast to the dominant thought of the day, which held that creation was evil or dirty, an afterthought or a mistake, to the God of Yisra'el creation was his best work. The Torah teaches us that creation lies at the heart of יהוה. It is his most heart-felt expression of love and graciousness. Throughout the creation process, recorded in Bere'shit chapter one, at the end of each "day", יהוה reviews his creation and sees that it is good. Again, in sharp contrast to pagan myth, in which man is usually a mistake or an after thought, man is יהוה's highest achievement.

> Bere'shit 1.26-31
> and יהוה had said, "let us make mankind in our likeness and like our semblance, and let them have dominion over the fish of the sea, and the flying things of the sky, and the beasts, and the whole earth, and all the creeping things that creep on the earth"; and יהוה had created mankind in His likeness, in the likeness of יהוה did He create it, male and female did He create them... and it was so; and יהוה had seen all that He had made and, behold, it was very good; and there had been evening and there had been morning, a sixth yom (day[3]).

3The word "*yom*" refers to a period of time. While the most common period of time it refers to is twenty-four hours, it is quite evident from Bere'shit that this is not referring to a twenty-four hour period of time because right after the seventh "*yom*", the whole seven-day period is considered a "*yom*". (Bere'shit 2:4).

Furthermore, יהוה is intimately concerned with and active in promoting the welfare of man, and mankind – even at the most basic level. In Jewish thought, יהוה is responsible for everything. Whether a woman is able or unable to have children is dependent on יהוה. Whether the rain falls to water the crops is dependent on יהוה. Whether a man will live or die is dependent on יהוה. Moreover, יהוה is not simply concerned with the welfare of man as a whole, He cares for each individual person.

> Tehillim 23
> A psalm of David.
> יהוה is my shepherd.
> I lack nothing.
> He causes me to lie down in grassy pastures;
> He leads me by restful waters.
> He restores my soul;
> He guides me in right paths
> as befits His name.
> Though I walk through a valley of deepest darkness,
> I fear no harm, for You are with me;
> Your rod and Your staff – they comfort me.
> You spread a table for me in full view of my enemies;
> You anoint my head with oil;
> my cup is well filled.
> Only goodness and loving faithfulness shall pursue me
> all the days of my life,
> and I shall dwell in the house of יהוה
> for a length of years.

The God of Yisra'el is יהוה alone, there are no other Gods. The God of Yisra'el is just, gracious and forgiving. יהוה, and יהוה alone was responsible for the creation of the universe, which was His greatest achievement, and man the crowning glory of that achievement.

The Torah Of Yisra'el

Our relationship with יהוה does not stop at the covenant He made with Avraham our father. It does not stop with His liberating us from Egypt. It starts there. The culmination of the expression of יהוה's love and compassion for us is our Holy Torah – the Teaching. The Torah, a perfect expression of יהוה's compassion, was given to Mosheh at Mount Sinai in an unprecedented encounter between יהוה and man.

A central tenet of our religion is the belief that יהוה is concerned about creation. יהוה was not content to establish creation, stand back, and observe it from afar. He is intimately involved with and concerned about the world He has invested so much of Himself in. The Torah is the ultimate expression of יהוה's concern for His creation. Through it, יהוה has reached out to us from beyond the gap of our incomprehension, to communicate his will in a concrete, unambiguous manner.

Our tradition teaches us that יהוה gave the Torah to Mosheh at Mount Sinai, who wrote all of it down. We learn this from the Torah itself.

Shemot 24.4
Mosheh then wrote down all the words of יהוה...

Shemot 34.27
And יהוה said to Mosheh: "Write down these commandments, for in accordance with these commandments I make a covenant with you and with Yisra'el ".

Devarim 31.9
Mosheh wrote down this Torah and gave it to the priests, sons of Lewi [Levi], who carried the Ark of the Covenant of יהוה, and to all the elders of Yisra'el
.

One very important belief of the Karaites is that the Torah of Yisra'el is complete as written.

> Devarim 4.2
> You shall not add anything to word that I command you or take anything away from it, to keep the commandments of יהוה your God that I command you.

Furthermore, the Torah is perfect:

> Tehillim 19.8
> The Torah of יהוה is perfect,
> restoring the soul;
> the testimony of יהוה is confirmed,
> Enwisening the simple.

Attached to the Torah are other books that comprise the Holy Scriptures, or Miqra'. These books are the Nevi'im, or Prophets, and Ketuvim, or Writings. When referring to the entire Bible, Jews often speak of the *TaNaKh*. This is an acronym for the three major sections or books of the Bible, the Torah [T], Nevi'im [N], and Ketuvim [K].

All together, the *TaNaKh* is comprised of 24 books. The Torah contains five books:

> Bere'shit (1),
> Shemot (2),
> Wayyiqra' (3),
> BeMidbar (4), and
> Devarim (5);

The Nevi'im contains eight books:

> Nevi'im Rishonim (Former Prophets):
> Yehoshu'a' (6),
> Shofetim (7),

Shemu'el Alef and Shemu'el Beit (8),
Melakhim Alef and Melakhim Beit (9)

Nevi'im Aharonim (Latter Prophets):
Yesha'yahu (10),
Yirmiyahu (11),
Yehezq'el (12)
Sheneim 'Asar [twelve "Minor" Prophets] (Hoshe'a',
Yo'el, 'Amos, 'Ovadyah, Yonah, Mikhah, Nahum,
Havaqquq, Sefanyah, Haggai, Zekharyah, and
Mal'akhi) (13).

The Ketuvim consists of ten books:

Tehillim (14),
Mishlei (15),
Iyyov (16),
Shir HaShirim (17),
Rut (18),
Eikhah (19),
Qohelet (20),
Ester (21),
Dani'el (22),
'Ezra' and Nehemyah (23),
Divrei HaYamim Alef and Divrei HaYamim Beit
(24).

The Ten Principles Of Faith

The heart of the Jewish experience, its blood and soul,
stems from our faith. Our sages, in their quest to understand and
provide a voice for that heart, formulated what they termed
principles of faith. These principles of faith were an attempt to
provide a framework for the basic beliefs upon which our
relationship with יהוה and His Torah are founded. The Ten
Principles Of Faith, ultimately codified by Eliyahu Bashyachi,
constitute a time honored understanding of what it means to be

Jewish from the perspective of faith. The Ten Principles of Faith, as defined by *Hakham* Bashyachi, are as follows:

1. The first principle states that everything that exists was created, except for יהוה. Prior to יהוה's creation of the universe, nothing but יהוה existed.

2. The second principle states that all creatures on earth have a Creator who, Himself, was not created. Thus, the existence of יהוה is the principle that underlies all others.

3. The third principle consists of three elements. First, יהוה bears no likeness to any creature on earth:

   Yesha'yahu 40.18
   To whom, then, can you liken יהוה, What form compare to Him?

   Secondly, יהוה is not material, but incorporeal, and this is so in spite of the physical activity we attribute to Him in such statements as He went up, He went down, He saw, etc. These are stated in human terms in order to facilitate our understanding of יהוה. Thirdly, יהוה is one:

   Devarim 6.4
   Hear O Yisra'el [Yisra'el], יהוה is our God, יהוה is one.

   We reinforce this concept of unity when we say: "One is our God, great is our Lord, holy and awe inspiring is His name for ever and ever".

4.   The fourth principle states that יהוה sent Mosheh on a mission to redeem the children of Yisra'el from their bondage in Egypt, and Mosheh fulfilled his mission with loyal devotion; he is the first and most important of the prophets; there has not arisen nor will there arise another prophet like him.

5.   The fifth principle states that יהוה gave Mosheh a single Torah, complete as written. This is the Torah that we possess to this very day. He forbade us to add to or remove anything from it:

Tehillim 19.8
The law of יהוה is perfect.

Devarim 4.2
You shall not add to the word which I am commanding you and you shall not diminish from it.

6.   The sixth principle states that we must know the language of our Torah, Hebrew, and its explanation. This is considered a requirement of the faith because every believer must be able to interpret Torah correctly in a manner that is in accord with the text.

7.   The seventh principle states that יהוה sent our prophets to communicate His will through them; however, our fathers failed to listen to the prophets. The result was the dispersion of Yisra'el from their land.

8. The eight principle states that there is an after life:

    Dani'el 12.2
    Many of those that sleep in the dust of the earth will awake, some to eternal life, others to reproaches, to everlasting abhorrence.

9. The ninth principle states that יהוה rewards a man according to his deeds, good or bad.

    Tehillim 11.5
    יהוה seeks out the righteous man,
    but loathes the wicked one who loves injustice.

10. The tenth principles states that יהוה has not turned away from His people in the Diaspora, nor has He forgotten them, even though they may not subject themselves to Him. Similarly, we should hope for the coming of our Messiah and for the coming of Eliyahu [Elijah] the prophet.

    Mal'akhi 3.23
    Lo, I will send the prophet Eliyahu [Elijah] to you before the coming of the great and awesome day of יהוה.

CHAPTER 2

The Roots of our People

The Name Karaite

We are called Karaites, or Children/Disciples of the Scripture (Benei Miqra' in Hebrew), because our faith is based on the written scriptures, and because our forefathers used to approach the Rabbanites with calls (qeri'ot) to uphold the commandments of the scripture.

The opinion most commonly held by the ancient Karaite Hakhamim is that the ancestors of the Karaites at the time of the Second Temple were the Saddiqim (Righteous) or Benei Sedeq (Children/Disciples of Righteousness/Truth). This name derives from the view that our faith is based on truth, and righteousness. Throughout the generations, our sages have vigorously rejected assertions made by some Rabbanites who regard Karaism as the continuation of the Sadducee sect (Sadduqim). Sadducees were Hellenists who held heretical views on faith, reward and punishment, the immortality of the soul, and the resurrection of the dead, which Karaites do not.

Opinions about the origin of the name Karaite differ greatly in the academic community. Some contend that the name predates 'Anan, others that it was assumed by a later coalition of movements that united under the attacks of Rabbanites leading up to Sa'adyah al-Fayyumi.

The Rise Of Karaite Judaism

Karaite Judaism – as a way of life, thought, and practice – dates back to the giving of the Torah. Karaite Judaism, as a reaction to the adulteration of the Torah, finds expression in the conflicts between many Second Temple sects. However, most scholars are in agreement that Karaism, as an organized movement, did not begin until the period following the destruction of the second Temple in 70 c.e. The story of the roots of our people, then, is the story of the second Diaspora, which begins with the story of the Jewish community in Babylon.

The Jewish community in Babylonia dates back to the time of the first Diaspora, detailed so vividly in the books of Mela'khim [Kings] and Yirmiyahu (amongst others). Most scholars date the beginning of the first exile around 586 b.c.e. During the reign of Cyrus ('Ezra' ch. 1), we were given permission to return to our homeland, and rebuild the Temple. Despite the return of many Jews to Yisra'el during this time, a substantial active community remained in Babylon. Following the second Diaspora, though the Jews scattered over the Roman Empire, many went to the community in Babylon for refuge. As it had been during the first Diaspora, Babylon, once again, became the major center of Jewish life.

The Arab conquests of the seventh century c.e. brought most of the Jewish world under the control and influence of Islam, including the Jewish communities in Babylonia. Under the Persian (Parthian and Sassanid) dynasties, the Jewish communities in Babylonia were self-governing and headed by an Exilarch, who represented the Jewish population before the king. Under Islamic rule, the Heads of the Rabbanite Academies (yeshivot) became increasingly powerful; they were known as Ge'onim ["exalted ones"]. The Exilarch was responsible for the collection of royal taxes; the Ge'onim for the administration of justice within the community. Both Exilarch and Ge'onim had under their authority an extensive bureaucracy of officials. Essentially, the Jews had a Jewish government, albeit under the state of the Muslims.

As a consequence of being under two governments, the greater Jewish population was subject to what amounted to double taxation: state taxes and communal taxes. Furthermore, there were additional taxes imposed by the yeshivot. To add to this, the Jewish population in Babylon was highly stratified. The landowners, bankers, and merchants made up the higher classes, while the farmers, laborers, craftsmen, and peasants comprised the lower classes. Typically, the lower classes were on the receiving end of the hardest of the hardships.

All during this period of time, the Mishnah and Gemara (Talmud) were being compiled and redacted. The authors of the Talmud – either literal or spiritual descendants of the Second Temple Pharisees, mostly (if not entirely) comprised of the ruling class – were mandating, as they had been doing in the land of Yisra'el, new forms of Jewish thought and observance. They forced these innovations, upon the Jewish people through their influence, now firmly rooted in the institutional authority of the Exilarch, the yeshivot, – and, by implication, the king.

As a result of the oppression felt by many Jews of the period, a portion of the population retreated to the outskirts of the community. Many of these Jews were motivated by their disagreements with the religious establishment, which they felt was overstepping its bounds. In fact, the earliest defining thread of most of the schismatic groups of this period was their rejection of the Talmud; and, it was out of these schismatic groups that the Karaites as a modern, organized movement formed.

One of the most influential of these early groups was the 'Ananites. Often confused with the first group of Karaites, because of the Rabbanite polemics against 'Anan, the 'Ananites strictly followed the teachings of 'Anan Ben-Dawid. A very ascetic sect, they were actually quite similar in many aspects to the Rabbanites ('Anan was quite heavily influenced by Rabbanism, and was criticized for this by later Karaite commentators, especially Dani'el al-Qumisi).

However, the 'Ananites were only one of the most prominent of the early schismatic groups. It was not until several generations after 'Anan that the Karaites were widely recognized as a formal Jewish movement.

The Golden Age Of Karaite Judaism

For a good period of time, there was a relative harmony between the Rabbanites and the Karaites. Granted, the Karaites were not approved of by the Rabbanite overlords; however the Rabbanite authorities were generally not concerned about them. The Karaites were perceived as nothing more than ineffectual pockets of dissent; and the Rabbanites believed they would soon disappear on their own, if left to themselves.

All of this changed in the ninth and tenth centuries, especially when Sa'adyah al-Fayyumi, an influential rabbi from Egypt, became the head of the Babylonian community. Sa'adyah was a very strong-willed man. He tolerated no resistance to his rule. In his mind, sufferance of any dissension was tantamount to approval.

In a series of polemic tracts, Sa'adyah systematically attacked Karaite practice and theology, falsely accusing 'Anan and the Karaites of nefarious intents and actions. The wake of the attack of Sa'adyah on Karaite Judaism caused a drastic change in the nature and construction of the Karaite communities. Prior to the ascension of Sa'adyah, Karaites and Rabbanites lived more or less side-by-side. This was to end. Prior to Sa'adyah, the Karaites had been little more than a confederation of like-minded schismatics. Now, they bonded together in self-defence. For example, in the ninth century. Dani'el al-Qumisi wrote:

> ... You will have no valid excuse before יהוה if you do not return to the Law of יהוה and to His ordinances as prescribed in it, because since the beginning of the Exile, in the days of the kingdom of the Greeks, the Romans, and the Magians, the Rabbanites held the offices of princes and judges, and those that sought the Law could not even open their mouths in behalf of the ordinances of יהוה for

fear of the Rabbanites who were [ruling over them].
Upon the arrival of the kingdom of Ishmael, however, matters improved, for the Ishmaelites always
help the Karaites to observe the true faith as set
forth in the Law of Mosheh, and we bless them for
it.

Now you who are living in the midst of the kingdom of Ishmael, which loves those who fix the new
moon by direct observation. Why, then, are you
afraid of the Rabbanites? יהוה will surely come to
your assistance. Arise, therefore, draw strength
from the Law of יהוה, strengthen ye hands that are
weak (Yesha'yahu 35.3), endeavor skillfully to
teach all Yisra'el the ordinances of יהוה and ad-
monish them with words of peace, not quarreling
and strife, as it is written: And they who have understanding among the people shall instruct
many... and many shall join them (Dani'el
11.33-34), this being a reference to the kingdom of
Ishmael, for with it יהוה broke the staff of the Rabbanites and removed it from over you".[4]

This period of travail for Karaite Judaism gave birth to a
rise in the quality of Karaite scholarship and an increase in the
literary output of its leaders. Instead of stamping out Karaite
Judaism, as the Rabbanites had hoped, their polemics served to
seal and solidify Karaite Judaism as a formal, organized movement. This period is known as the Golden Age of Karaite Judaism.

The Golden Age of Karaite Judaism lasted from the tenth
century through 1200 c.e. In it, much of the works of the great
Karaite luminaries such as Ya'aqov al-Qirqisani, Yefet Ben-'Eli
HaLewi, Sahl Ben-Masli'ah, Yosef al-Basir, Yeshu'ah

---

4 Translation from Leon Nemoy's, *Karaite Anthology*, p. 39f, Yale University
Press, 1952.

Ben-Yehudah, Salmon Ben-Yeruam and others were produced. Their legal codes, commentaries, grammars, lexicographies, translations, and poetry are still widely respected and relied upon to this day. Their works are filled with discourses on science, philosophy, medicine, world religions, and other topics that display their vast knowledge and erudition.

This period of time saw the rise of the Shoshanim (Heb. for lilies, a reference to Hoshe'a' 14 and Tehillim 69 and 80), or Avelei Siyyon (Mourners of Zion, see Yesha'yahu 61.3). During the eighth century, the beginnings of the migration of many members of the Karaite community back to Yerushalayim began, among them Dani'el al-Qumisi. The community grew to such size and stature that, in the tenth century, Yerushalayim became the recognized center of scholarship for Karaite Judaism. This community was typified by its absolute rejection of the Diaspora – theologically, physically, and legally. They were ascetics, who believed that it was incumbent upon all Yisra'el to lament for the destruction of the Temple, until it was restored. Furthermore, they believed that any life outside of the land of Yisra'el was a violation of the Torah.

Karaites from Byzantium, Spain, North Africa, Iraq, Persia, and other reaches of the exile travelled to Yerushalayim and studied with the Avelei Siyyon. When they returned, these students brought back with them the commentaries, legal codes, and translations they had acquired. In this way, the learning of the academies was disseminated to the community as a whole.

What follows is a brief introduction into some of the most formidable minds of this period, and their works, namely: Ya'aqov al-Qirqisani, Yefet Ben-'Eli HaLewi, and Sahl Ben-Masli'ah.

Ya'aqov al-Qirqisani is often regarded as one of the greatest minds of Karaite Judaism, medieval or otherwise. In the course of his lifetime, he produced at least ten works of which we are aware. He wrote an exhaustive legal code, commentaries, philosophical works and polemics, as well as works on philology, interpretive methodology, grammar, the nature of witchcraft, medicine, dream interpretation, psychophysiology, natural science, etc.

Qirqisani's most famous works are the Kitabu 'r-Riyad wa-'l-Hada'iq (Book of Gardens and Parks), a commentary on the non-legal portions of the Torah and the Kitabu 'l-Anwar wa-'l-Maraqib (Book of Lights and Watchtowers), a systematic code of law. It is in the Book of Lights and Watchtowers that Qirqisani made one of his most valuable contributions to the modern study of Karaite Judaism: a concise record Karaite Judaism's history.

Ya'aqov al-Qirqisani's other works include: Tafsir Bere'shit, a commentary on Bere'shit, Tafsir Qohelet a commentary on Qohelet, Kitab Fi 'Ifsad Nubuwwat Muammad a polemic against the pseudo-prophecies of Muhammed, al-Qawl 'Ala 't-Tafsir wa-Sharhu 'l-Ma'ani a treatise on the art of textual interpretation, al-Qawl 'Ala 't-Tarjama an essay on the art of translation, and Kitabu 't-Tawid a philosophical work on the oneness of יהוה.

Yefet Ben-'Eli HaLewi, a native of Basra, Iraq, is considered the foremost Karaite commentator of the Golden Age of Karaite Judaism. He lived in the last half of the tenth century, through the first part of the eleventh. Like Qirqisani, he wrote only in Judæo-Arabic. Yefet Ben-'Eli's commentaries cover the breadth of scripture: Torah, Nevi'im, Ketuvim; and each commentary is presented with his own translation of the biblical text. Occasionally, Yefet Ben-'Eli includes in his commentaries information about grammar, history, and law, or polemics against the Rabbanites; however, he tends to remain focused on his task of explaining the text at hand.

Though Yefet was a formidable scholar, his commentaries are not necessarily the product of original thought. His genius comes out in the synthesis of his learning and in its application. He drew heavily upon both Rabbanite and Karaite scholars before him; and he makes no pretensions to the contrary. Yefet's commentaries have enjoyed great popularity and hold a strong influence in both Karaite and Rabbanite communities to this day.

Little is known of the life of Sahl Ben-Masli'ah. He was a contemporary of Yefet Ben-'Eli HaLewi, and a resident of Yerushalayim. Sahl was a prolific writer, who composed a legal commentary (*Sefer HaMiswot*) among many other writings. However, his chief contribution to modern Karaite scholarship is his letter to Ya'aqov Ben-Shemu'el. What is interesting, and revealing about this letter is the insight it provides into Karaite missionary tactics. Much of the material that has been passed down to us today that relates Karaite propaganda is directed to the upper classes of Rabbanite society – the educated and erudite. The letter of Sahl Ben-Masli'ah was directed at a general audience – the man on the street, as it were. Furthermore, it highlights many important historical facts, such as information about Karaite leaders and descriptions of the Rabbanite customs and superstitions of the day.

The Golden Age of Karaite Judaism, was the coming of age of the Karaites. It was during this period that some of our most important literature, literature that has contributed greatly to the intellectual heritage of Judaism worldwide, was written. The attacks of Sa'adyah, rather than our death toll, were just our birth pangs.

Karaite Judaism In Byzantium

The Karaites from Byzantium, who came to the Yerushalayim academies to study, transcribed, translated, and summarized the teachings of the Yerushalayim masters into Hebrew for their communities at home, who spoke Judæo-Greek. Their efforts resulted in a major center of Karaite study, which would become the seat of the Karaite academy, after the destruction of Yerushalayim in 1099 by European crusaders. The most important of these early scholars are Tuvyah Ben-Mosheh, and Yehudah Hadasi.

Tuvyah Ben-Mosheh studied with Yosef al-Basir, and translated his writings. He also compiled an enormous commentary on Wayyiqra', entitled Osar Nehmad – of which we have one volume extant today. Yehudah Hadasi, composed the encyclopædic Eshkol HaKofer, which was a repository of almost all earlier Karaite learning.

Often difficult to read, and far from original, these works were only partially successful in preserving and promoting Karaism. However, they remain important in the fact that they provided some level of access to the heritage of the Yerushalayim academy.

From the thirteenth century, through the fifteenth century, the Karaites in Byzantium laboured to maintain Karaite scholarship. Great efforts were put forth to maintain the scholarship that had existed up to that time, while at the same time producing new works.

During this period, as well, a strong Rabbanite influence began to make itself felt in Karaism. The writings of Avraham ibn-'Ezra and Maimonides [Mosheh Ben-Maimon] had a profound impact on the Jewish communities of the Mediterranean; and the Karaites were not exempt from their sway. The rational, philological bent in the writings of ibn-'Ezra (including Yefet Ben-'Eli HaLewi's influence on him), and the rational philosophy of Maimonides attracted many Karaites. This despite the harsh, anti-Karaite tone of many of his early works.

Aharon Ben-Yosef and Aharon Ben-Eliyahu were two of the most outstanding Karaite scholars of this period; and the Rabbanite influence on them is apparent. Their works frequently cite Rabbanite authors by name, such as RaShI [Rabbi Shelomo Ben-Yishaq], Dawid Qimhi, Nahmanides [Mosheh Ben-Naman], and the two aforementioned ibn-'Ezra and Maimonides, sometimes in favor, most often in conflict.

The Karaite *Hakham* Eliyahu Bashyachi is perhaps the most famous and controversial scholar of the Byzantine period. He, and his brother in-law Kalev Afendopolo, composed the legal commentary Aderet Eliyahu, which continues to have a deep impact on Karaite observance to this day. Bashyachi was also, perhaps, the scholar most profoundly influenced by Rabbanism. He went to the extent of suggesting that Avraham ibn-'Ezra was a student of Yefet Ben-'Eli; and that when ibn-'Ezra attacked the

Karaites, it was out of fear that it would be discovered his true sympathies were Karaite.

Bashyachi's popularity is most likely due to the fact that his code was made widely available in Russia. It became popular in Egypt, when Russian Hakhamim began to lead the community there.

The influence of Rabbanism at this time cannot be understated. It was so pervasive that some Karaites even engaged in philosophical allegory and the study of Qabbalah – endeavors vehemently opposed by their predecessors, and forbidden by the Torah.

The Karaite Jews Of Eastern Europe

During the reign of Theodosios I (398 c.e.), Karaites from Persia moved to Adrianople (the modern Edirne, Turkey) in the Byzantine Empire – eventually, gradually moving from there to Constantinople (the modern Istanbul, Turkey) and also to the Crimean peninsula, settling in the city of Sulkhat, called presently [in Karaite Judæo-Tatar] Eski Kirim ("Old Crimea"), being that the Crimean peninsula had recently come under Byzantine control.

Under the Byzantine emperor Constantine V (Circa 742 c.e.), Khazar Turks from the region of Bukhara invaded the Crimea. Karaite writers in Byzantium and elsewhere deride the Khazars, call them enemies of Yisra'el , and even equate the name Khazar with the Hebrew word "mamzer" (see Ya'aqov Ben-Re'uven's [11th - 12th century c.e.] *Sefer* Ha'Osher as well as the commentaries of Yefet Ben-'Eli HaLewi [10th century c.e.] and Yeshu'ah Ben-Yehudah [11th century c.e.]).

At the end of 11th century c.e., The crusader Baldwin I, Count of Edessa and King of Yerushalayim, with the aid of the Genoese, transferred 250 Karaite families from Yerushalayim to the Crimea, settling them in the fortress towns of Qale [Chufut-Kale] and Mangup. Circa 1200 c.e., Tatars conquered the interior of the Crimea. The Genoese founded trading colonies on the coast. Many more Byzantine Karaites moved to the Crimea. The

Judæo-Greek speaking Karaites gradually adopted the language of the Tatars and developed the Karaite Judæo-Tatar dialect. The Tatars esteemed the Karaites so well that the Khan appointed a Karaite to the hereditary title of Agha and mint-master. This position remained until the Crimea was conquered by Russia in the late 18th century.

Grand Duke Witold Jagello of Lithuania, after defeating the Tatars in a war in the Crimea, in 1388 c.e., exiled 483 Karaite families from Sulkhat [Eski Kirim] and settled 330 families in Trakai [Troki], near Vilinius, and the remainder he settled in the town of Paneveys. After Witold united Lithuania with Poland (1392 c.e.) he warred again against the Tatars who had invaded from the Crimea into Poland. He took an additional 280 Karaite families from Sulkhat [Eski Kirim] and settled 180 of them in Galicia in the city of Halicz on the Dnester river and the remainder he settled 200 families in Volhynia in the city of Krasna Góra on the hill across the Styr river opposite the fortress city of Luck (Lutzk). From there Karaites spread to other towns in Lithuania, Volhynia, and Podolia. Some time after the deportation of the 763 Karaite families from Sulkhat [Eski Kirim], the remaining Karaites moved from Sulkhat [Eski Kirim] to Kaffa (Kefe) [Feodosia], Qale [Chufut Kale], Mangup, and Gozlov [Evpatoria], thus ending the Karaite settlement in Sulkhat [Eski Kirim].[5]

In 1463 c.e., Turks conquer the Crimean coast ousting the Genoese, the Karaites remaining in the fortress towns, except in Mangup where Tatars settled as well among them[6]. Later, due to oppression by the Arnauti[7], the Karaites fled Mangup and went to Qale [Chufut-Kale] and to Gozlov (Evpatoria). After the Karaites fled Mangup, the Tatars also abandoned it. Sometime after the Karaite community of Luck had grown greatly, another

---

5 Information pertaining to the settlement of Karaites by Grand Duke Witold is derived from Mordehai Sultanski's Zekher Saddiqim, which is sometimes cited for inaccuracies and anachronisms; however, it remains the one of the only accounts of the early Karaite settlements in Eastern Europe.

6 It is generally not known that the Crimea was a major center of Armenian culture during this era. Major monasteries were built there where significant manuscripts were copied.

7 Related to the Turkish "Arvanut", which means Albanian.

community of 60 families was started at Derazne (Derazhno) in Volhynia near Luck on the Hory river. That community was, however, destroyed by the Ukrainian Haidamak leader Gonta's army and the few survivors returned to Luck and Halicz.

The Karaites in Lithuania also spread out and settled in many towns such as Pasvalys (Poswol) [in the region of Panevezys], Salaty and Posalaty [in the region of Panevezys], Birzai (Birze) [in the region of Panevezys], Seda (Szaty) [in the region of Telsiai (Telz) or Ukmerge (Wilkomir)], Kronie [in the region of Trakai (Troki)], Swiate Ozero, etc.

A number of Karaite families were transferred by the Polish King Jan Sobieski III from Trakai [Troki] to Kukizow [Krasne Ostrow], in 1688 c.e. Over 100 years later, after Galicia came under Austrian rule, due to oppression by the local governor, the majority of Karaites abandoned Kukizow [Krasne Ostrow] and went to Halicz and Luck. Between 1783 and 1795 c.e., Russia conquered and annexed the Crimea and Lithuania.

During the reign of Empress Catherine II of Russia, the Karaites petitioned the crown to relieve them of the double tax that was imposed on all Jews. Catherine granted their request, and permitted them to acquire land (which had been denied to other Jews). Despite this grant, legislative decrees still referred to the Karaites as Jews. 1827 – 1840 c.e., Russian Tsar Nicholas I exempted Crimean Tatars and Karaites from the general military draft law. The same exemption was extended to the Karaites of Lithuania and Volhynia. The official Russian designation for the Karaite Jews was changed from "Jews-Karaites" to "Russian Karaites of the Bible Faith". The Karaites were put on an equal footing with the Muslims and were granted an independent church statute (this made them no longer responsible to the Rabbanite communal authorities for the collection of taxes and recognized the independence of the Karaite Beit Din).

In 1863 c.e., The Karaites were given rights equal to those of the native Russian population. Through 1874 c.e., the Office of the *Hakham* in Evpatoria, in an effort to relieve the Karaites of some of the oppressive Russian anti-Semitic laws, convinced the Russian government, that they were not Jews, but the descendants of the Turkic Khazars. This was only for external consumption. Within the Karaite community they continued to identify themselves as Jews.

Due to increasing anti-Semitic laws and actions, in order to protect the rights of the Karaite community, in 1910 c.e., the congress of Hakhamim and Hazzanim decided to no longer allow marriages between Rabbanites and Karaites or accept Rabbanites who wished to become Karaites (This ban was not always followed, and marriages between Rabbanites and Karaites still occurred, but rarely).

After the Bolshevik revolution, 1917 c.e., the Communist government accepted the Tsarist opinion that the Karaites were a Turkic people descended from the Khazars. Due to the anti-religious policies of the Communist regime, almost any teaching about the Jewish heritage of the Karaites ceased and most Karaites in the U.S.S.R. began to believe the Khazar ruse.

In 1940 c.e., Lithuania was annexed by the U.S.S.R. and Poland became a Soviet satellite. Communist policies were extended to those countries as well, and the same result occurred as in the U.S.S.R.

After the fall of the Soviet Union, 1993 c.e., Karaites in the former U.S.S.R. and Poland began to show a renewed interest in their Jewish heritage, some even emigrating to Yisra'el .

The Karaite Jews Of Egypt

The history of the origins of the Karaite community in Egypt remains somewhat of a mystery. We do know that Karaite communities were founded in Alexandria and Fustat in the early part of the ninth century. During the early years of the Karaite settlements in Egypt, the Karaites and Rabbanites lived in relative harmony from what we can tell. We have no records that indicate any major conflicts between the two groups despite their significant religious disputes. In fact, to the contrary, we have documents that detail marriage between Rabbanites and Karaites.

Beginning in the period of the Tulanid dynasty (868-969c.e.), the Karaites began to gain influence in the Islamic court. This is evidenced by the power of the Yerushalayim community during this period of time. At this period, we also begin to see struggles that formed between the Rabbanite and Karaite communities. In 1024 c.e., Caliph az-Zahir issued a formal decree prohibiting the oppression of Karaites, presumably not without cause.

The Fatamid dynasty (969-1171 c.e.) was generally favorable to Jews. Consequently, the Karaite communities in Egypt flourished during this period. These conditions continued under Salah ad-Din, who overthrew the Fatamid dynasty in 1171 c.e. Salah ad-Din established the Ayyubid dynasty, which lasted from 1171-1250 c.e. Importantly, when Salah ad-Din captured Yerushalayim, he helped the Karaites reclaim the codex of Ben-Asher the Masorete[8]. This important document remains in our possession to this day.

With the rise of the Mamluks in 1250 c.e., the Ayyubid dynasty came to an end. Unlike the three dynasties that preceded them, the Mamluks were not favourable to the Jews. During the fifteenth century after the discovery of the trade route to India, Egypt 's œconomy suffered great losses. To compensate for this, the Mamluk government imposed heavy taxes on the Jewish population.

In 1517 the Islamic world was overtaken by the Ottoman Turks. With their ascendancy conditions improved for the Jews – for a time. The Ottoman empire from its very beginning was noted for its weak central government. This fault would ultimately be its downfall. The most immediate consequence of this for the Jewish population, however, was that their former Mamluk governors remained in power despite the change in dynasty.

The first real change in policy towards the Jews in Egypt since the Mamluk rise to power came when Muhammad 'Ali

---

8 The Masoretes were a group of Karaite scholars, among whom the Ben-Asher family was the most prominent. The Masoretes preserved the authoritative text of the TaNaKh.

(Mehmet Ali), an Albanian officer in the Turkish army, became the governor of Egypt in 1804. He put a permanent end to any form of Mamluk government, and instituted many social and œconomic reforms that benefited the community.

In 1882 Egypt became a protectorate of the British Empire. Under the rule of the British, the condition of the Jews and other non-Muslim groups in Egypt improved dramatically. This era marked a renaissance in the life of the Egyptian Karaite community. At the time when Muhammad 'Ali assumed control of Egypt, there were approximately fifteen hundred Karaites in the land. In 1952, this number had grown to almost five thousand.

The Karaite community in Egypt continued to flourish well into the 1960s. With the Arab Yisra'el i war of 1967, the community in Egypt came to an abrupt end. Many members of the community were taken hostage and put in concentration camps, others fled for their lives. Synagogues were officially closed. For the most part, though there remain a few scattered Karaites in Egypt to this day[9], the Karaite community dispersed. The majority of the community settled in Yisra'el , others settled in France, while the remaining members who left were sponsored by the Jewish Federation of San Francisco; these members established a community in San Francisco that is still in extant today.

Karaite Judaism Around The World Today

Karaite Jews in Yisra'el

The largest community of Karaites in the world today exists in Yisra'el. Rough estimates of the number of Karaites in Yisra'el range from 30,000-40,000. The community is comprised mainly of refugees from the Islamic revolution in Egypt, but it also contains the entire Karaite community from

---

9 At present there are under ten (10) Karaites living in Egypt, most of whom are very old.

Hit in Iraq, and six Karaite families from Tunisia, Turkey, and Eastern Europe. The community in Yisra'el is the seat of Universal Karaite Judaism (the organisation of the Karaite Jewish Community in Yisra'el), the Karaite Beit Din, and the *Hakham* Rashi (the chief religious leader of Karaite Judaism in Yisra'el).

Some of the more prominent communities in Yisra'el are in Ramlah, Ashdod, and Ofaqim. Ramlah and Ashdod are the primary centers of administrative activity, given that the religious councils preside there (the Religious Council, the Council of Hakhamim, and the Beit Din). Others are Be'ersheva' [Beersheba], Ranen, Masli'ah, Bat Yam, Yerushalayim, and 'Akko [Acre].

Karaite Jews in Europe

Between World War I and World War II, the center of East European Karaism was under Polish rule. In 1932, Seraja Szapszal, was elected *Hakham* Rashi / Ulu *Hakham* (leader) of the Polish Karaites. Professor Szapszal was a vehement public supporter of the myth that Karaites were not Jews, but descended from Khazars.

At the beginning of World War II, when the Soviet Union annexed the Ukraine and Lithuania in 1939-1940, all the Karaites who had been living in the Russian and Austro-Hungarian empires found themselves now living under one state, the Soviet Union. Initially, this change in governmental status had no effect on the community; however, after the Germans occupied Lithuania and the Ukraine, the *Hakham* of Trakai, became the de facto and de jure head of all East European Karaites.

During World War II, due to the successful efforts of the Karaite authorities over the last 100 years and the help of certain Rabbanites, the Nazis did not perceive the Karaites to be Jewish, and, therefore, they were, for the most part, except for a few places, left unscathed by the Holocaust.

In 1959, there were approximately 5,700 ethnically identified Karaites in Eastern Europe. As of 1994, the number had dwindled to 280. In 1953, under Soviet rule, the Kenesa [the Karaite Judæo-Tatar word for synagogue, derived from the Hebrew Beit Keneset] in Panevezys was closed and nationalized. In 1970, it was destroyed. The Kenesa in Vilnius was nationalized and reconstructed in 1949. It was returned to the Karaites in 1988, and reopened in 1993.

For a time, beginning in the 1970s, and due to the efforts of Professors Ananiasz Zajaczkowski and Alexander Dubinski, there was a rise in the activity of the Karaites in Eastern Europe. In 1974, a dictionary of Karaite Judæo-Tatar (the language of European Karaites) was published in Moscow. In 1988, with the revival of national cultures in Lithuania, the "Lithuanian Karaim Culture Community" was established as a formal organization supporting ethnic Karaites. In 1992, a united "Lithuanian Karaim Religious Community" was established, with Mikolas Firkovich elected as its President and *Hazzan* (leader of the community). In 2000, Mikolas Firkovich died; and with him, essentially, the religious organization of the Karaite communities of Lithuania and Poland.

A small community of Karaites still exist in the Crimea; however, their numbers are fading fast as well. Most of these Karaites, however, consider themselves to be Turkic or Tataric first and Karaites culturally or ethnically.

Karaite Jews in the United States

Karaite Jews began emigrating to the United States in reasonable numbers during the middle part of the past century, around the 1950s (though Karaites from Eastern Europe and Turkey had immigrated in small numbers as early as the late 1800s and early 1900s). As noted, the Islamic revolution in Egypt, and the tensions between Egypt and Yisra'el that occurred during those years, marked the end of Jewish communal life in Egypt.

One of the earliest émigrés to America was, Ya'aqov Masli'ah. He came to San Francisco California, by way of Paris, in 1957. Mr. Masli'ah, who worked hard at building and organizing the community, may be considered the founding member of the Karaite Jews of America.

Perhaps the most significant event in the history of the Karaite community in the United States was the sponsorship of several Egyptian Karaite refugee families by the San Francisco Jewish Federation. Almost all of the families in the American Karaite community today come from the families who were sponsored by the San Francisco Federation.

Other significant events include the establishment of the Karaite Jews of America as a formal, body in the 1980s, along with the purchase of the first synagogue, which was actually a residence, in the same time period. The second synagogue was purchased from a defunct Reform congregation in the mid-1990s.

Today, there are approximately 600 Karaite families living in the United States. Of those, approximately 400 live in California, within a reasonable distance from the Daly City synagogue. While the seat of the Karaite Jews of America is in Daly City, its membership is continent-wide, serving members in Canada as well as the US. There are large communities of Karaites in Chicago and Los Angeles, and a number of Karaites live in the states of New York and Rhode Island, and the province of Quebec; however, the only Karaite synagogue in the United States at this time is located in Daly City. At the time of this writing, another Karaite congregation - Orah Saddiqim, in upstate New York - is in the process of founding their synagogue.

Karaite Jews in other places

There are approximately 1,000 Karaites in Turkey (mostly in and around Istanbul). There are still some Karaites in Iran; however, due to the present state of affairs in Iran, we are unable to communicate with them to ascertain their numbers. Until the end of the 19th century the was a Karaite community in Chinese Turkestan that had existed there since at least the 9th century.

As noted above, there were still some Karaites in Tunisia as late as 1948, when six Karaite families were registered as having immigrated to Yisra'el from there.

After the Bolshevik Revolution a number of Karaites from Crimea and the Ukraine moved to Harbin in Manchuria. There are a number of Karaites from Turkey, Yisra'el, Manchuria, and Eastern Europe that have settled in Australia. There are a number of Karaites from Egypt and from Eastern Europe that have settled in France (chiefly in Paris) and some individuals that have settled in Switzerland, Belgium, Great Britain, and Italy.

CHAPTER 3

Halakhah: A Way of Thought

A Different Mind Set

'Anan HaNasi', *Sefer* Miswot
The Merciful One has ordered us to perform his precepts with awe and reverence, as it is written: "Worship יהוה with awe". (Tehillim 2.11)

Halakhah, is translated most often as "law". In Hebrew it literally means, "walking", or "going". It is a play on words. *Halakhah* implies a journey, a life-path. This choice of words is designed to imply that the Torah is not just a set of laws, but a way of life, and a perspective on life. *Halakhah* is encompassing, life enveloping and life transforming.

As a perspective on life, the *Halakhah* contains certain assumptions about life: about יהוה, man, nature and their interrelationship.

Halakhah assumes certain things about יהוה. It assumes the existence of יהוה. It assumes that יהוה is active in the events of the world and the lives of men. It assumes that יהוה is responsible for man.

Halakhah assumes certain things about man. *Halakhah* assumes that men require formal boundaries. It assumes that men and women are different, and should be treated differently. It assumes that men may be stratified into classes, and that different classes of men may be treated differently: the 'Eved (bond servant), for example, does not have all the rights of a free

45

man; and the elderly should, by the fact of their age, be respected. It assumes that man is accountable to יהוה.

Halakhah assumes certain things about nature. It assumes that nature may be assistant to the will of man. It also assumes that man has a significant responsibility to maintain nature for יהוה, and that a balance between the two must exist. It assumes that there is a life force that animates things. It assumes that the land is significantly impacted by how that life force is managed. It assumes that life in nature at all levels is precious, and should not be wasted. It assumes that all of creation is intimately connected with the actions and will of man and יהוה.

Halakhah is not forgiving. יהוה is forgiving. *Halakhah* is not lenient. יהוה is lenient. This is an important differentiation to keep in mind. While יהוה, throughout the *TaNaKh*, again and again, forgives the people of Yisra'el, he does so to the injury of His rights under *Halakhah*; *Halakhah* remains uncompromising. Even in the case of an inadvertent transgression, the *Halakhah* does not provide for legal lenience or stay of guilt.

> Wayyiqra' 4.2-3
> "Speak to the children of Yisra'el , saying: 'If a person sins unintentionally against any of the commandments יהוה [in anything] which ought not to be done, and does any of them… then he shall offer to יהוה for his sin which he has sinned…

> BeMidbar 15.22-27
> If you sin unintentionally, and do not observe any one of these commandments which יהוה has spoken to Mosheh… then it will be, if it is unintentionally committed, without the knowledge of the congregation, that the whole congregation shall offer one young bull as a burnt offering, as a pleasing aroma to יהוה, with its grain offering and its drink offering, according to the ordinance, and one kid of the goats as a purification offering… And if a person

sins unintentionally, then he shall bring a female goat in its first year as a sin offering.

While *Halakhah* is uncompromising, it is not impossible and discompassionate. It is not deaf to the struggles of the poor and destitute. Much more than many other legal systems, *Halakhah* strives to enable and facilitate the participation and inclusion of all people.

Wayyiqra' 5.5-11
And it shall be, when he is guilty in any of these [matters,] that he shall confess that he has sinned in that [thing;] and he shall bring his guilt offering to יהוה for his sin which he has committed, a female from the flock, a lamb or a kid of the goats as a sin offering. So the priest shall make a covering over for him concerning his sin. If he is not able to bring a lamb, then he shall bring to יהוה, for his guilt which he has sinned, two turtledoves or two young pigeons: one as a purification offering and the other as an 'Olah... But if he is not able to bring two turtledoves or two young pigeons, then he who sinned shall bring for his sacrifice one-tenth of an 'Efah of semolina as a purification offering. He shall put no oil on it, nor shall he put frankincense on it, for it [is] a purification offering.

See also, Wayyiqra' 14.19-21, and Wayyiqra' 27.1-8.
Halakhah is, in fact, uncompromising about compassion. In *Halakhah*, there is little (if any) separation between compassion and justice. *Halakhah* requires compassion; it legislates compassion. In the mind of *Halakhah*, the lack of compassion is a very serious transgression.

Shemot 22.22
You shall not afflict any widow or orphan.

Wayyiqra' 19.13
You shall not cheat your neighbor, nor rob [him.]
The wages of him who is hired shall not remain
with you all night until morning.

Devarim 24.20-21
When you beat your olive trees, you shall not go
over the boughs again; it shall be for the stranger,
the orphan, and the widow. When you gather the
grapes of your vineyard, you shall not glean [it] af-
terward; it shall be for the resident alien, the orphan, and the widow.

Devarim 27.19
Cursed [is] the one who perverts the justice due
the resident alien, the orphan, and widow. And all
the people shall say, 'Amen!'

One of the most significant obstacles modern Westerners face when coming to the Torah is the contrast between their
philosophy and the philosophy of the *Halakhah*. Notions in
Halakhah regarding sexual and marital relations, often conflict
with Western mores, for example, polygyny.

Shemot 21.7-11
If he takes another [wife,] he shall not diminish her
food, her clothing, or her conjugal rights.

Remedies and dicta of *Halakhah* are often distasteful to
modern Western morality.

Shemot 21.17
And he who curses his father or his mother shall
be put to death...

Halakhah must be embraced for what it is. It cannot be explained away, or made palatable to a modern sensibility. It has been a significant mistake of many commentators to attempt to apologize for *Halakhah*. The *Halakhah* needs no apology. What is required on the part of those faced with a conflict between their beliefs, and the *Halakhah* is a determination on their part of the truth. One must ask oneself, "Where does the truth lie? Is it in my beliefs, or those of the *Halakhah*?" If it is determined that truth lies in *Halakhah*, then other methods of thinking must be abandoned. Again, this is the most significant obstacle the majority of modern Westerners face when coming to the Torah.

Belief And Practice

Historically, there has been a tension between faith and practice in Judaism, which continues to this day. Karaism, for a long period of time, though not classically, has contended that faith is the most important element of our religion. In the world of the European Karaites the focus on faith was preeminent. To quote a European Karaite author, Simon Szyszman:

> Faith alone determines the adherence of an individual to Karaism. He who believes in the great affirmation of this religion, regardless of his origin and his particular racial or religious ethnic affiliations is considered to be a Karaite. Similarly, faith alone is the indispensable condition which assures salvation, not the accomplishment of commandments and rights.

While it is true that faith is a very important element of our religion, any cursory glance at the Torah, the foundation of our religion, will show that faith alone is not enough (this is the realm of Christianity). Our model for the man of faith is Avraham Avinu [Abraham our Father]. Avraham was a man of faith and a man of observance; in him we find, perhaps, our truest example of the man of *Halakhah*.

In faith, Avraham left everything he knew to travel to the land of Yisra'el on a promise from יהוה. Strictly obedient, Avraham carefully observed the covenants he made with יהוה. What we learn from him is that יהוה requires both faith and observance, and that יהוה respects and holds dear the man who can find a synthesis of them in his life. One without the other is a life lived out of balance, out of step with the teachings of the Torah.

Methods Of Interpretation

Traditionally, there are three ways of interpreting the Torah: direct reference from the written scripture, inference from aspects of the written scripture, and traditions about interpretation of the written scripture.

Direct Reference

Direct reference is a plain reading of the text. It is very simple. We strive to interpret the Torah as it requires itself to be interpreted.

Where appropriate, we understand the Torah literally. Where appropriate, we understand the Torah figuratively. We do not add anything to the Torah, or take anything from it.

> Ya'aqov al-Qirqisani, Kitabu 'r-Riyad wa-'l-Hada'iq
> ...Scripture as a whole is to be interpreted literally, except where literal interpretation may involve something objectionable (i.e., absurd), or imply a contradiction.

Inference

Inference is the act or process of deriving logical conclusions from premises known or assumed to be true. It is a procedure that combines known facts to produce ("infer") new facts. Inference relies upon simple logical syllogisms to arrive at its conclusions. For example, consider the following, which uses the logical rule "modus ponens":

> Socrates is a man.
> All men are mortal.
> Therefore, we can infer that Socrates is mortal.

Examples of inferences are:

> Wayyiqra' 20.19
> You shall not uncover the nakedness of your mother's sister or of your father's sister, for he [who does so] has laid bare his one own flesh-relative; they shall bear their guilt.

From this we infer that just as a man may not marry his father's or his mother's sister, so may a woman not marry her mother's brother or her father's brother.

> Shemot 16.26-29
> Six days you shall gather it [the manna]; on the seventh day, the Sabbath, there will be none... Let every man remain in his place, and not go out from his place [encampment] [to collect the manna].

From this we infer that we may not gather or harvest on the Sabbath.

Traditional Custom

There are laws in the Torah that are given without explaining concretely how to fulfill them. Our ancestors developed methods for observing these laws. These are our customs. While we respect our customs like we respect the laws of Torah, it is very important to remember that a custom may not contradict the Torah. Any custom that is found to contradict, add to, or detract from the Torah must be abandoned.

Examples of where traditional custom has further defined a practice are:

> <u>Circumcision</u>: The Torah does not state explicitly how a circumcision is performed. Consequently, we have an ancient tradition that dictates the procedure of a circumcision

> <u>Ritual Slaughter</u>: The exact manner of ritual slaughter is not fully described in the Torah; therefore, the method has been passed on traditionally. Tradition tells us that the only place where we can kill an animal in accordance with the Torah, so that it's blood be spilled out and the animal die immediately, is at the neck where we can sever the carotid arteries and jugular veins.

> <u>The Piercing of Meat and Removal of Blood</u>: The Torah tells us that we may not eat any blood. Consequently, we attempt to remove blood from any meat that is slaughtered. This must be done in an appropriate amount of time so the blood does not clot. Piercing Meat is one way of ensuring that the blood is removed quickly. We learn this from tradition. The same tradition tells that any method of cooking that does not allow the blood to drain from the meat as it's being cooked is also forbidden.

Halakhah, then, is both explicit and interpretive. It may be derived directly from the text, or through the text. Furthermore, our understanding of carrying out the laws of the Torah is enhanced by the traditions derived from Torah that have surrounded its observance through the ages.

Practices Not Observed And Why

There are several practices we are commanded to observe that require the presence of the Temple for their observance. Without the Temple, we are required to refrain from observing them. The list below, though not exhaustive, mentions some of those practices:

- Separation of Dough (Hafrashat Hallah)

- Redemption of the First Born (Pidyon HaBen)

- Tithing (Ma'aser)

- Pilgrimage to the Temple (Hagh)

The Daily Way
of Life

CHAPTER 4

Righteousness

Kindness

Wayyiqra' 19.18
And you shall love your fellow as yourself: I am יהוה.

Zekharyah 7.9-10
Thus has יהוה of hosts said: "Judge with true justice, perform loving faithfulness and compassion each person to his brother. And do not oppress the widow and the orphan, the resident alien and the poor, nor shall you think evil in your heart, anyone against his brother".

In the *TaNaKh* kindness is not an impulse that we should follow when we have been possessed by its spirit. Kindness is a way of life; it is something that should stand out as a defining aspect of who we are. Being kind, developing a kind heart and mind, should be a life-long goal for every Jew. This kindness and respect should express itself in all our actions.

Avraham, our father, was a pillar of kindness. The Torah teaches us that he graciously welcomed strangers and travelers into his home, providing them with repast, shade, and comfort. He showed intimate concern for his immediate family's welfare, and for his extended family.

59

Bere'shit 18.1-8

Then יהוה manifested Himself to him by the oak trees of Mamre, and he was sitting in the opening of the tent at the hot part of the day. So he lifted his eyes and looked, and behold, three men were standing nearby to him; and he saw and he ran from the opening of the tent towards them, and bowed down to the ground. And he said, "My lords, if I have now found favor in Your sight, pray do not pass away from Your servant. Pray let a little water be brought, and wash your feet, and recline under the tree. And I will bring a morsel of bread, that you may refresh your hearts. After that you may pass by, inasmuch as you have come to your servant". They said, "Do as you have said". So Avraham hurried into the tent to Sarah and said, "Quickly, make ready three Se'im of semolina flour; knead [it] and make round loaves". And Avraham ran to the herd, took a tender and good calf, gave [it] to a young man, and he hastened to prepare it. So he took butter cream and milk and the calf which he had prepared, and set [it] before them; and he stood by them under the tree as they ate.

The passage above is a wonderful example of the extent to which Avraham would go to be kind. In it, he sees what he perceives to be three weary travelers. He rushes to meet them, gives them honor (by bowing at their feet), and offers to provide them with a simple respite from the heat. He does much, much more than this, however. He prepares them a magnificent meal, and waits attentively on them as they eat it. How much more should we be kind to our own families, if this is the example set by Avraham to strangers?

What follows are a few of the laws of kindness.

Husbands must be kind to their wives, and wives their husbands (Shemot 21.10).

A nation must not rob a woman of her husband by taking him off to war when she has been newly wed (Devarim 24.5).

We are required, if we find something that has been lost, to try to return that object to its owner (Devarim 22.1-4).

We are prohibited from despising someone in our community (Mishlei 14.21).

We are commanded to be merciful, to love mercy (Mikhah 6.8).

Charity

Devarim 15.7
If there is among you a poor man of your brethren, within any of the gates in your land which יהוה your God is giving you, you shall not harden your heart nor withdraw your hand from your poor brother...

Charity is an aspect of kindness. However, in the eyes of the Torah, charity is so important that it deserves special attention in and of itself. For Jews, charity is a part of our essence. The Torah prescribes the following laws of charity:

We are required to provide loans to other Jews without charging interest (Shemot 22.25, Wayyiqra' 25.36, Devarim 23.19-20).

During the *Shemitah* [sabbatical year of release] and the *Yovel* [Jubilee year] we are required to forgive loans we have made to other Jews; and we are forbidden from failing to give someone a loan because we know the *Shemitah* [sabbatical year of release] or the *Yovel* [Jubilee year] is coming soon, or at hand (Wayyiqra' 25.1-55, Devarim 15.1-18).

We are required to take a portion of our income and provide for the needs of the poor in our community (Devarim 26.12-13).

We are required to provide for the upkeep of our religious organizations (BeMidbar 18.21).

We are required to contribute to the redemption of other Jews who are being ransomed [from being kidnapped, taken prisoner, or enslaved] (Wayyiqra' 25.47-55).

Slander, Vengeance, Deception

Slander, vengeance, and deception are things the Torah takes very seriously. When Miryam [Miriam] and Aharon [Aaron] in their jealously of Mosheh spoke out against him, Miryam [Miriam] was punished with *Sora'at*[10] (BeMidbar 12.10). Many Jewish thinkers have felt that one must be so careful not to accidentally slander someone that they ruled one must refrain from speaking about an individual if they are not present. This is not a prescription of the Torah; however, it demonstrates the seriousness of this issue.

The Torah makes it very clear, that vengeance is forbidden to us. It is qadosh (set aside, reserved) for יהוה. At the same time, we must not mistake vengeance with justice. While we are prohibited from taking vengeance, we are required to pursue justice. If we have been wronged, what we must do is ensure that we do not take justice into our own hands, but allow the appropriate communal structures to achieve our justice for us.

---

10 *Sara'at* is usually mistranslated as "leprosy".

Deception is often the thread that ties slander and vengeance together. In a case where a malicious witness falsely testified against a defendant, and it was found out, the punishment he or she sought for the defendant will be dealt to them (Devarim 19.16-21). If a man falsely accuses his wife of not being a virgin when they got married, he will be forced to pay a fine and is barred from ever divorcing her (Devarim 22.13-19). What follows are some of the laws relating to slander, deception, and vengeance:

> We are forbidden to lie, unless someone's life is at stake.

> We are forbidden from taking vengeance (Wayyiqra' 19.18).

> We are forbidden from slandering and maligning someone's character (BeMidbar 12).

Work And Wages

In ancient Yisra'el ite society the wage-earning class, known as hired laborers, would be known as day laborers today. They were entirely dependent on their daily earnings for their subsistence. This explains why they are associated with the widow, orphan, and resident alien. Given their low œconomic state, these day laborers could be easily exploited. Therefore, the Torah requires that hired servants receive their wages promptly:

Wayyiqra' 19.13
You shall not oppress your fellow, nor rob him. The wages of a hired laborer shall not remain the night with you until morning...

Devarim 24.14
You shall not oppress a hired laborer, a poor and needy person, whether one of your brethren or one

of the resident aliens who is in your land within your gates. Each day you shall give him his wages, and not let the sun go down on it, for he is poor and has set his heart on it; lest he cry out against you to יהוה, and it be a sin in you.

Yirmiyahu 22.13
O one who builds his house without righteousness and his upper chambers without justice while his fellow (the laborer) works for nothing and his wages are not given to him...

Mal'akhi 3.5
"And I will come near you for judgment; I will be a swift witness against sorcerers, and against adulterers, and against perjurers, and those who oppress the hire of hired laborers and widows and orphans, and against those who turn away an resident alien and do not stand in awe of Me", says יהוה of hosts.

Wages could also be considered unacceptable by virtue of the way they were acquired. For example, wages earned through prostitution could not be offered at the sanctuary:

Devarim 23.19
You shall not bring the gift of a prostitute or the price of a dog [a euphemism for a male prostitute] to the house of יהוה your God for any vowed offering, for both of these are an abomination to יהוה your God...

Animals

All of יהוה's creation is important. Throughout the creation story in Bere'shit 1, the Torah tells us that יהוה saw his creation was good. In Bere'shit 1.22, יהוה singles out the animals and blesses them. From this the Torah teaches us that animals are valued by יהוה for themselves. Animals are not primarily created for the benefit of humanity, and deserve respect because they are a part of יהוה's precious creation.

יהוה has given mankind control over animals (Bere'shit 1.28; cf. Tehillim 8.6-8). This control is in actuality a responsibility. We are caretakers of the animals יהוה has created. In the beginning, we were not permitted to eat animals (Bere'shit 1.29). It was only after our decline that יהוה allowed us to eat animal flesh; and from that time forward, animals have feared us.

Bere'shit 9.2
And the fear of you and the dread of you shall be on every beast of the earth, on every bird of the air, on all that move on the earth, and on all the fish of the sea...

There are a number of laws that concern the welfare of animals, some of which are:

The Sabbath rest applies equally to animals (Shemot 23.12; cf. Wayyiqra' 25.7; Devarim 5.14).

An ox treading the grain must not be muzzled (Devarim 25.4).

A fallen ox must be helped to its feet (Devarim 22.4; cf. Wayyiqra' 22.27-28; Devarim 22.6-7, 10).

The *TaNaKh*'s sense of responsibility for the welfare of animals is summed up well in Mishlei:

Mishlei 12.10
A righteous man knows [to care for] the life of his animal.

Acts Of Justice

Justice is a part of the essence of יהוה. It is one of his primary concerns. In large part, it is an extension of his concern for the helpless. The victims of injustices are disproportionately from the poor, among whom are the orphan, the widow, and the resident alien. יהוה sets the standard for justice, by which we must judge ourselves. He cannot be bribed nor does He pervert justice in any way.

> Devarim 10.17
> For יהוה your God is the superlative God and superlative Lord, the great, mighty, and awesome יהוה, who shows no partiality (in judgement) nor takes a bribe.

> The following are some of the laws regarding justice.

> We must practice justice in business transactions (Way-yiqra' 19.35-36; Hoshe'a' 12.7).

> The righteous must never show partiality in judgement to the rich (Devarim 24.17) nor to the poor (Wayyiqra' 19.15).

> We are forbidden from testifying along with a majority that we know to be unjust (Shemot 23.2).

> We are required to appoint just men as judges over our communities (Devarim 16.18).

Ritual Items - *Sisit* And *Tallit*

The commandment of *sisit* and *Tallit* first appears in the book of BeMidbar:

BeMidbar 15.37-39
And יהוה said to Mosheh saying: "Speak to the Children of Yisra'el and say to them they shall make for them-selves fringes [Sisit] on the corners of their garments throughout their generations; and they shall place plaited cord of blue [Petil Tekhelet] upon the fringe [Sisit] of the corner and it shall become a fringe[Sisit] for you. And you shall see it and remember all the com-mandments of יהוה. And you shall do them. And not stray after your heart and after your eyes, which you whore after".

It also appears in Devarim:

Devarim 22.12
You shall make braids [Gedilim] on the four corners of your covering garment with which you cover yourself.

The clothing here referred to is called, in Biblical Hebrew, a *simlah* (it is called a *Tallit* in Mishnaic Hebrew), from the root S-M-L, to wrap or envelope (cf. the Arabic word "shamla" [cloak])[11]. The *simlah* was a universal-covering garment, used by both men and women. It was, essentially, a sheet-like cloak (like the Turkish çarşaf). Men and women's *simlot* (plural of *simlah*) were differentiated by style. For the poor, the *simlah* served as both clothing and a blanket with which they covered themselves while sleeping. (see Bere'shit 9.23 and Shemot 22.26)

Although the Torah does not specify the type of material to be used in fulfilling this commandment, our tradition recommends that the fringes [sisiyot (plural of sisit)] be made of luxurious material (see *Sefer* Aderet Eliyahu, 'Inyan HaTefillah, *Pereq Shevi'i*).

---

11 In modern Hebrew the word is misapplied to a woman's dress.

Similarly, the fringes [*sisiyot*] have to be made in two colors, white and blue: "and they shall place a plaited cord of blue [petil *Tekhelet*] upon the fringe [*sisit*] of the corner" is the principle command. Traditionally, we have made the garment (*Tallit*) white. *Tekhelet* blue is the color of the sky. The two materials are braided together[12] from end to end, half of them white and half of them blue, ending in two fringes, one white and one blue. The sages also enjoined that the fringes [*sisiyot*] be visible, on account of the words: "that you may see it". The provision is given so that יהוה's commandments be remembered and fulfilled and a person avoid committing any transgression.

This commandment is incumbent upon all: men, women, boys, girls. The blind person is not exempt from wearing *sisiyot*, even though he himself cannot see them, for he is obliged to let others see it so that the commandment "and you [plural in Hebrew] shall see it" will be fulfilled.

The Prayer Shawl (Tallit)

With the passing of time, the design of garments have changed. In general, people no longer wear four cornered covering garments (with the noted exception of a scarf). In order to preserve the commandment of the *sisit*, therefore, it has become a custom to wear a *Tallit* (*simlah*) at significant religious events (prayer, circumcision, etc.,).

Before donning the *Tallit* the wearer recites this blessing:

Barukh Atah יהוה Eloheinu Melekh Ha'Olam Asher Qiddeshanu BeMiswotaiv WeSivvvanu LiLbosh Arba' Kanfot BaSisit: Amen.

12 Braids: Gedilim. The only other place where the word "*Gedilim*" is used in TaNaKh is a description of chain-work braids that adornered the Temple of Solomon (Melakhim Alef 7:17. Similarly, in Arabic, the word *Jadil* means a braid, as in the hair, as does the Aramaic word *Gadila*.

Blessed are you, יהוה our God, Ruler of the universe who has sanctified us with his commandments and commanded us to wear four cornered garments with the *sisit. Amen.*

Forbidden Mixing

Sha'atnez

Devarim 22.11
You shall not wear *Sha'atnez* [a type of cloth combining wool and linen together].

Sha'atnez (an Egyptian loan word) is a cloth made of a mixture of wool and linen. Why is that the only cloth that is forbidden? It was used by Egyptian priests in their idolatrous worship. Such a material may not be woven, nor may such materials be sewn together (sewing being considered the same thing as weaving, in sewing you are weaving a single thread through multiple threads). Combinations other than *Sha'atnez* are generally permitted; furthermore, it is permitted to wear a woolen garment over a linen garment, or the reverse.

Interbreeding different species of animals

Interbreeding, such as a horse with an ass, ram and goat, he-goat and roe-deer, etc., is prohibited; nor may a man allow others to interbreed animals. This rule is applied by inference to fowl and fish also. This also applies to interbreeding humans and other animals (as in bestiality):

Wayyiqra' 18.23
And with any animal, you shall not have carnal relations with any beast to defile yourself with it;

and do not let a woman stand before a beast for it
to mate with her; it is a violation of nature.

Mixtures of seeds [from different species]

In addition to the passage from Wayyiqra' quoted at the
head of this section, the Torah also forbids crossing heterogene-
ous species of plants:

Devarim 22.9
You shall not sow your vineyard with seeds from
different species, lest the entirety be proscribed –
both the seed which you are sewing, and the yield
of the vineyard.

At the same time, the crossing of two varieties of the
same species is permitted, as for example, "delicious" and
"Jonathan" apples; green and red grapes; green and red figs; or
two varieties of parsley.

If interbreeding occurs in nature then we are not prohibited from benefiting from the results. What we are forbidden
from doing is actively engaging in interbreeding ourselves, as
discussed above.

'Avodah Zarah

'Avodah Zarah, literally translated, means foreign worship; it includes activities such as idol worship, and belief in, or
service/worshipping of created things, for example: an angel, the
sun, the moon, the stars, light, darkness, the wind, wood, stone,
fire, etc.

Shemot 20.3-5
You shall have no other gods besides Me.
You shall not make for yourself a sculptured im-
age, and any likeness of what is in the heavens

above, or on the earth below, or in the waters under the earth. You shall not bow down to them or
serve them. For I יהוה your God am a zealous God,
punishing the guilt of the parents upon the children, upon the third and upon the fourth generations of those who hate Me.

Devarim 4.15-19
And you shall guard your souls well. For you did
not see any form on the day that יהוה spoke to you
on Horev [Horeb] from the midst of fire. Lest you
act corruptly, and make yourself a sculpted image
whether the image of a symbol, the image of a male
or a female – the image of any animal, of any
beast, which is in the land – the image of any bird,
of anything that creeps on the ground. And lest
you raise your eyes to the sky and see the sun and
moon and the stars, all the host of the sky, which
יהוה formed for all the peoples under all of the
heavens, and you cast yourself down and bow
down to them and worship them.

Similarly, the Torah makes frequent warnings to us not
to follow or believe in any kind of 'Avodah Zarah:

Wayyiqra' 19.4
You shall not turn to false gods or make cast images of gods for yourselves: I יהוה am your God.

Wayyiqra' 26.1
You shall not make false gods for yourselves, or set
up for yourselves sculpted images or standing
stones[13], or place *Maskit* stones[14] in your land to
worship upon, for I יהוה am your God.

---

13 Idolatrous peoples often set these up to stand in for their gods – this is not an
image, but a simple stone that served to represent a god.

Devarim 7.5
Only thus you shall do to them: you shall tear down their altars, smash their standing stones, cut down their *Asherim*[15], and you shall burn their images in the fire.

It is also written:

Devarim 7.25
You shall burn the sculpted images of their gods in the fire; you shall not covet the silver and gold on them or keep it for yourselves, lest you be ensnared thereby; for it is an abomination to יהוה your God.

The Torah warns us against nine abominations associated with *'Avodah Zarah*. These are:

- Passing son or daughter through fire.

- Augury.

- Observing the sky for signs in the clouds.

- Divination.

- Sorcery.

- Charms.

- Consultation with spirits and familiars.

---

14 These stones were horizontal instead of vertical; they were carved with images upon which the worshipper bowed.
15 These were sacred posts or trees that were used alongside an altar to represent a fertility god (as in the standing stone).

- Necromancy – asking for signs or information from the dead (Devarim 18.10).

- Writing by etching on the flesh (tattooing, branding, gashing, scarification, etc.,) (Wayyiqra' 19.28).

All types of occult activities, and anything derived from them, are idolatrous and are forbidden. Examples are:

- Fortune telling (phrenology, palmistry, tea leaf reading, coffee ground reading, astrology – any form, tarot card reading, etc.,).

- Object consultation (Ouija boards, Pendulums, sticks, animals, etc.,).

- Crystals and talismans (such as the khamsa, or hand of Fatimah).

- Research into *'Avodah Zarah*.

- Entry into places where *'Avodah Zarah* is practiced, such as a church.

- Shaving the hair so that only the center of the hair is left (as Egyptian priests did and the Hindus do), or so that the center of the hair is bald (as with Franciscan monks).

- Men cannot destroy the edges of their beards (but they may trim them [Wayyiqra' 19.27]).

- Cross-dressing: a man may not wear clothing or jewelry meant for a woman. So, too, a woman is forbidden from wearing a man's clothing, accessories, or implements of war (guns, swords, etc.,). (Devarim 22.5).

We are also forbidden to buy or sell objects connected with 'Avodah Zarah, to give or receive them, to deal with them in any manner (other than their destruction).

Enticement and Proselytization

One of the most heinous crimes detailed by the Torah is enticement to 'Avodah Zarah. Anyone guilty of this crime is liable to the death penalty. The Torah considers it so important, it states:

> Devarim 13.7-10
> If your brother, your own mother's son, or your son or daughter, or the wife of your bosom, or your closest friend entices you in secret, saying, "Let us go and worship other gods" – whom neither you nor your fathers have known – from among the gods of the peoples around you, either near to you or distant, from one end of the earth to the other: You shall not assent and you shall not listen to him; and you shall not have pity nor shall you have any compassion for him, nor shall you conceal him; for you shall kill him, your hand shall be the first against him to put him to death; and the hand of the rest of the people thereafter.

If an entire city was guilty of turning to 'Avodah Zarah, that city would be consigned to the flame; all its possessions, including livestock, would be destroyed, burned and proscribed. The city is to never be built again. Nothing may be taken from it. It must remain an eternal ruin, serving as a reminder of what the city had done, and what its punishment was.

In the modern age, where we are under governments that do not permit us to fulfill this commandment, we must treat anyone who attempts to entice us to *'Avodah Zarah* as if they were dead, shun them, and have no dealings with them. This applies to father, wife, son, daughter, etc. In our eyes, this person must not exist.

> 'Anan HaNasi', *Sefer* Miswot
> Since we no longer issue death sentences when someone commits a sin requiring capital punishment, we must separate ourselves from him. If it is a man, we must separate his wife from him; it if is a woman, we must separate her husband from her. We must not converse with the culprit or let him dwell with us or engage in doing business with him; neither borrow anything from him, nor lend to him; neither accept charity from him nor show any pity toward him. In short, we must treat him as if he were dead.

Kibbud Zaqen (Honoring The Aged)

> Wayyiqra' 19.32
> You shall rise up before a hoary head and shall pay honor to the face of an elder.

> Mishlei 16.31
> Gray hair is a crown of glory;
> It is found in the path of righteousness.

The root of the Hebrew word for honor (kavod) literally means to be heavy or weighty. The figurative meaning, however, is far more common: "to give weight". To honor someone implies a level of gravity. It implies that we must take them seriously.

While honor is an internal attitude of respect, courtesy, and reverence, appropriate attention or even obedience should accompany it. Honor without such action is incomplete. It is lip service (Yesha'yahu 29.13).

The manner of honoring the old:

- Rise in their presence (Wayyiqra' 19.32).

- Go forward to greet them.

- Walk with them, and accompany them.

Hakham Yefet Ben-'Eli HaLewi said: "Whoever is senior in the community must be respected; his words must be heard and he must be honored".[16]

Oaths

An oath is, essentially, a declaration or assurance given to indulge in or refrain from some specific form of activity, or a testimony. Oaths can be either written or oral. They can be temporary in nature or made binding for the indefinite future. The declaration may be sealed by a gesture, such as a simple handshake, or a formal written document. More complicated undertakings may need ratification by witnesses.

Oaths are serious undertakings made between people of good will and solemn intent, in the expectation that the promise inherent in the oath will come to fruition as intended by the participants. Among the most serious of the divine commandments is that forbidding the taking of a false oath in יהוה's name. A false oath is made by an individual that has no intent of keeping the promise they declare. It can also be an oath made without the solemn intent necessary to ensure its credulity, or false testimony. An oath made in יהוה's name is one where the person utilizes the name of יהוה as a means of communicating the severity of their intent or the veracity of their testimony.

---

16 This only applies if the person follows Torah, and his words do not contradict it.

The prohibition of making a false oath is the third of the Ten Pronouncements[17], given us at the time of the giving of the Torah by יהוה at Sinai:

> Shemot 20.7
> You shall not swear falsely by the name of יהוה your God; for יהוה will not clear one who swears falsely by His name.

This prohibition includes oaths invoking any of the appellations of יהוה (or an inference to יהוה), in addition to the four-letter name יהוה. Swearing on the Creator, or the Most High, is just as forbidden as a false oath sworn on the actual name יהוה.

The Name Of God

> Aharon Ben-Eliyahu, Sefer 'Es Hayyim, Chapter 74
> The Divine name consisting of the letters Yod He' Waw He' is called by the sages: the four letter name [Tetragrammaton]. This is the name of God's essence; it is the most elevated of all the appellations ascribed to God, and is described by the sages as the name applied exclusively to God... For this reason it is called HaShem HaMeforash, i.e., this name is distinguished and set apart (meforash) exclusively for God.

יהוה, also known in English as the Tetragrammaton (from the Greek meaning "that which is written with four letters") because of its four letters, is, strictly speaking, the only proper name for our God. It is also the most frequent name used for God in the TaNaKh. יהוה is used 6,828 times (almost 700 times in Tehillim alone). יה, a shortened form, appears fifty times in the TaNaKh, including forty-three occurrences in Tehillim,

---

17 Commonly called the Ten Commandments; however, there are many more commandments than just ten.

often in the exclamation "Hallelu-Yah" (lit. praise יה). It also exists a myriad of times in names in the beginning as Yeho- and the end as either -Yah or Yahu (for example, Yehosedeq, Yehoshefat, Eliyahu, 'Ovadyah, Shemayahu, etc.,).

We are warned, very sternly, in the Torah to respect the name יהוה. Anyone who blasphemes יהוה's name is subject to very serious punishment.

Wayyiqra' 24.13-23
And to the Children of Yisra'el you shall speak saying: "Any person who curses (Meqallel) his God shall bear his guilt; and a person who reviles (Noqev) the name of יהוה, shall be put to death. The whole community shall stone him; whether resident alien or native born. For his reviling (Noqev) the name, he shall be put to death.

This does not entail, as is obvious from the fact that the name of יהוה is used frequently in Hebrew personal names, that use of יהוה's name is forbidden. Our Torah, and our tradition are very clear on this matter:

Aharon Ben-Eliyahu, *Sefer 'Es Hayyim*, Chapter 70:
Since we find that יהוה applies names to Himself and it is proper for Him to ascribe names to Himself, it is likewise proper for us; for the ascription of names either by Him or by us is for the same purpose, namely, to make known to others His will by the ascription of a particular name. If the ascription of names were withheld from us it would also be withheld from Him without distinction.

What the Torah dictates is that we are forbidden from <u>cursing</u> יהוה's name. The words the Torah uses are meqallel – curse, and noqev – revile/blaspheme. Implicit in the reviling of

יהוה's name is a reviling of יהוה Himself, and this is the root of this miswah.

Those familiar with English translations of the Torah, often misunderstand this commandment because the passage containing it has been intentionally mistranslated. For example, the word noqev: The New JPS translation (1988) reads:

> If he also pronounces (noqev) the name of יהוה, he shall be put to death...

In contrast the Old JPS (1917) edition reads, accurately:

> And, he that blasphemeth (noqev) the name of יהוה, he shall surely be put to death...

This translation is in line with all other major *TaNaKh* translations, such as:

> RSV: He who blasphemes the name of יהוה ...

> NKJV: And he that blasphemes the Name of יהוה ...

> NASB: Moreover, the one who blasphemes the name of יהוה ...

The New Brown Driver Briggs Hebrew and English Lexicon contains the following entry from N-Q-V:

> 5344 II Verb: Curse (perhaps related to the root for piercing); Wayyiqra' 24.16.

This is further illuminated by the fact that the Torah clarifies its meaning further in the following passage:

> BeMidbar 15.30
> And the person who acts with a high hand (i.e., intentionally), whether native born or resident

alien, blaspheming (*gadaf*) יהוה and that person shall be cut off from the midst of his people.

Very clearly, then, what is at issue in the Torah is not the pronunciation of the name of יהוה, but rather the cursing, blaspheming, or reviling of the name of יהוה. Contempt for יהוה's name is the same as contempt for יהוה. This is precisely why the Torah takes this matter so seriously, and assigns the death penalty to it.

Given the severity of this prohibition, many Karaites have refrained from pronouncing the name of יהוה at all. While this is an understandable practice, the true intent of the Torah should not be forgotten. Others have maintained that to not pronounce the name in reading the *TaNaKh*, in prayer, or in taking an oath and to substitute other words for it is itself forbidden and blasphemous.

Ya'aqov al-Qirqisani, Kitab 'l-Anwar wa-'l-Maraqib, Book I, Chapter 19.4
Some of the Karaites of Khorasan ignore *Ketiv* and *Qere* and read only what is written. Some of them do so in the case of the Name which is written *Yod He'* [*Waw He'*], and maintain that he who reads it as *Alef Dalet* [*Waw Nun Yod*] is an unbeliever.

CHAPTER 5

Laws of *Tum'ah* and *Tahorah*

There are no English equivalents to translate the Hebrew words *Tahor* and *Tame'*. The closest one can come for these states is "pure" and "impure", respectively. Many moderns think that the laws of *Tum'ah* and *tahorah* are simply primitive health regulations that have become obsolete with the advent of modern health practices. There is no question that some of the laws are beneficial to health. However, health is not the reason for the Torah laws of *Tum'ah* and *tahorah*. We learn the reason from the Torah:

> Wayyiqra' 20.25-26
> You shall differentiate between animals that are *tahor* and those that are tame', between birds that are tame' and those that are *tahor*, and you shall not make yourselves abominable by beast or by bird, or by any kind of living thing with which the earth swarms, which I have differentiated to you as unclean.

> Devarim 14.21
> You shall not eat anything that has died [of itself] ... for you [are] a holy people to יהוה your God.

We are required to be *tahor* because we are required to be holy. To be holy means to be set apart, marked as different, spiritually elevated. These laws have defined us and set us apart

81

to this day. This is the reason for the laws of *Tum'ah* and *tahorah*, and no other.

The ordinary state of most things is *tahor*. However, anything can become tame' in a variety of ways: skin diseases, discharges of bodily fluids, touching something dead (BeMidbar 5.2), or eating tame' foods (Wayyiqra' 11; Devarim 14).

A tame' person is not permitted to touch or be in the presence of holy things, and it is incumbent upon them to ensure that they return to a state of *tahorah*, to the extent possible. Choosing to remain tame', or ignore the laws of *Tum'ah* and *tahorah* is a violation of the Torah (Wayyiqra' 5).

The Torah requires us to be *tahor*, and nowhere does the Torah dictate that this requirement is dependant on the Temple (Wayyiqra' 17.16; BeMidbar 19.12-13). Even those who contend that the laws of *Tum'ah* and *tahorah* no longer apply still observe some of the laws of sexual and animal *Tum'ah* and *tahorah*. Certainly, with the existence of the Temple one must be even more careful about their purity status, but this does not mean that without the Temple *Tum'ah* and *tahorah* do not matter. We see, for example, that *Tum'ah* lead to the expulsion of the Cana'anites from Yisra'el (Wayyiqra' 18.25). Certainly one cannot contend that this had anything to do with their relationship to the Temple in Yerushalayim.

Understanding that the purpose of the laws of *Tum'ah* and *tahorah* is to make us holy provides an insight into the nature and purpose of holiness. The physical practices associated with laws of *Tum'ah* and *tahorah*, are meant to provide us with a foundation that will enable us to elevate our selves morally, intellectually, and spiritually. A few examples will illustrate this point. Eating meat torn by wild beasts is dehumanizing; it reduces people to the level of scavengers (Shemot 22.31). Cooking a kid in its mother's milk is a perverse act, a pagan (Cana'anite) fertility rite (Shemot 23.19; 34.26; Devarim 14.21). Leaving the corpse of an executed man exposed on a tree (or gallows) overnight is barbaric (Devarim 21.23). Those involved in a war, even at the command of יהוה, become tame' (BeMidbar 31.19-24). Laws concerning sexual relations encourage self-control and stigmatize violators (such as prostitutes) as social outcasts and criminals. The prohibition of consuming blood is directly related in the Torah to a respect for life. Furthermore, one was only permitted to kill an animal if it was for food; then, only certain animals were permitted, if specific procedures were followed. If killing animals is not trivial, how much more serious is it to kill a person?

The laws of *Tum'ah* and *tahorah* prohibit integrating worship with sexuality. This is in stark contrast with Christianity and the pagan religions which revel in sexual imagery of the believer's relationship with their god. In the mind of the Torah, sexual acts make one tame', and therefore, unfit to enter the presence of יהוה.

Tahorah (Purification)

Methods of *tahorah* vary with the severity of the *Tum'ah*. The most serious to least serious cases in descending order are:

1. Skin disease (Wayyiqra' 13-14).

2. Childbirth (Wayyiqra' 12).

3. Genital discharges (Wayyiqra' [Wayyiqra' 15.3-15,28-30).

4. The corpse-contaminated priest (Yehezq'el 44.26-27).

5. The corpse-contaminated Nazirite (BeMidbar 6.9-12).

6. One whose *Tum'ah* is prolonged (Wayyiqra' 5.1-13).

7. The corpse-contaminated layperson (BeMidbar 5.2-4; 19.1-20).

8. The menstruating woman (Wayyiqra' 15.19-24).

9. The handling of the ashes of the red heifer or the *Yom HaKippurim* sacrifices (Wayyiqra' 16.26, 28; BeMidbar 19.7-10).

10. Seminal emission (Wayyiqra' 15.16-18).

11. Contamination by a carcass (Wayyiqra' 11.24-40; 22.5).

12. Secondary contamination (Wayyiqra' 15; 22.4-7; BeMidbar 19.21-22).

Tahorah almost always involves waiting a period of time[18] (until the following evening for minor cases, and as much as eighty days for the birth of a daughter); and, aside from ordinary washing with sweet water (i.e., potable water, as opposed to salt water or contaminated water), could also involve ritual washing initiating *tahorah*, atoning sacrifices, and priestly rituals. Practically, in the absence of an active Temple, the process of *tahorah* involves two things: a waiting period, and ritual washing in sweet water. For more detailed information on the required *tahorah* for specific cases, see the section on the corresponding *Tum'ah* below.

Animal *Tum'ah* And *Tahorah*

Most of the laws categorized in Torha law as the dietary laws, or laws of kashrut, are more accurately referred to as the laws of animal *Tum'ah* and *tahorah*. The fact that these laws significantly affect the diet has given rise to their connection with

---

18 There is one exception as noted in this chapter relating to the tumah of fæces.

dietary regulation, but it is important to note that these laws extend far beyond the table. Consequently, in Karaism, we do not speak of *Kasher*, or *Kosher* (a Yiddish pronunciation of the Hebrew word), we speak of *tahor* and tame' – unless we are speaking colloquially.

Understanding that the dietary laws are an extension of the laws of animal *Tum'ah* and *tahorah*, we better understand why we observe them. We observe the laws of tumah and *tahorah* to maintain our holiness (as above). We are required to be a holy people, and by refraining from eating tame' foods, we keep ourselves from being defiled.

General Rules

Although the details of animal *Tum'ah* and *tahorah* laws are extensive, they all derive from a few, simple principles:

> Certain animals may not be eaten or used at all. This restriction includes the flesh, skin, horns, hair, organs, eggs, and milk of the forbidden animals.

> Any food that has come in contact with any part of the carcass of a tame' animal becomes tame' and is forbidden (Wayyiqra' 7.19).

> All animals that may be eaten must be slaughtered in accordance with Torah law. Very simply, this entails that all blood must be drained from the animal and covered with earth (Be'reshit [Genesis] 9.4, Devarim 12.16, etc.,).

> Certain parts of the permitted animals may not be eaten (i.e., Be'reshit [Genesis] 32.32 Wayyiqra' [Wayyiqra' 3.17, 7.23-24).

Animals in specific states and relationships may become tame' if slaughtered (i.e., Wayyiqra' 22.28).

Permissible and Prohibited Foods

Note: It is important to note that the following sections are merely an introduction to the details of the laws of animal *Tum'ah* and *tahorah*, and their implications. Except as noted below, whole foods[19] of vegetable origin that are *tahor* present no issues.

The Torah classifies animals in three categories based on their characteristics. It does not differentiate between animals as we do, i.e., mammals, reptiles insects, etc. The three main categories used in the Torah are land animals, water animals, and flying animals. It further categorizes land animals and differentiates between mammals, and creeping animals (reptiles, amphibians, insects, etc.,). Beyond this, with the exception of the winged animals, the Torah provides general criteria for determining the purity status of a given class of animal (i.e., land, water, etc.,).

We may eat any mammal that has cloven hooves and chews its cud (Wayyiqra' 11.3; Devarim 14.6). Any mammal that does not have both of these qualities is forbidden. The Torah specifically forbids the camel, hyrax, hare, and pig because they are missing one of these signs.

Of the water animals, anything that has both fins and scales while it is in the water is permissible (Wayyiqra' 11.9; Devarim 14.9). Thus, sharks, sturgeon, shellfish such as lobsters, oysters, shrimp, clams and crabs are all forbidden. Fish like tuna, carp, salmon, and herring are all permitted. As for fish that are born with fins and scales but loose them while still in the water (i.e., before being caught), they are forbidden. However those than shed their scales when they are removed from the water are permitted.

---

19 The term "whole foods of vegetable origin" is used to indicate foods that have not been processed: i.e., a whole apple vs. apple sauce, or a whole wheat berry as opposed to flour.

There are no criteria for flying animals. The Torah lists specific forbidden flying animals (Wayyiqra' 11.13-19; Devarim 14.11-18). We do not know the names of some of the animals on this list. Their meaning has been lost to us over the ages. The only flying animals we do know are *tahor* are those that were used for sacrifices in the Temple (doves/pigeons and turtle-doves) and the quail; and there is a dispute among Karaite scholars whether these are permitted without the Temple (c.f. 'Anan HaNasi' *Sefer* Miswot IV.1, Dani'el al-Qumisi *Sefer* Miswot I.5-7). Of the birds considered *tahor*, both 'Anan HaNasi' and al-Qumisi mention the Dove/Pigeon (*Yonah*), and Turtledove (*Tor*).

> Dani'el al-Qumisi, *Sefer* Miswot
> Now, you must know that we are not at liberty to eat of any birds until we shall have learned the precise meaning of these names of forbidden birds. Yet, who is there today who knows the significance of these names of forbidden birds? Rather, one person says thus-and-thus, while the other person says it is not so. Such of these names as also occur elsewhere in Scripture we are able to interpret with fair certainty; for example, the crow and the eagle. Others, which occur nowhere else in Scripture, we cannot identify at all; for example, the peres, the 'ozniyah, the tahmas. The Hebrew language has ceased being spoken among us, and we no longer know which birds these terms signify.

Of the "winged swarming things" (winged insects, etc.,), a few are specifically permitted (Wayyiqra' 11.22) – several species of locust and grasshopper; all others are forbidden.

The carcass of any tame' animal (which includes improperly slaughtered animals) transmits *Tum'ah* (Wayyiqra' 11.32-40). Generally, we may not use any part of these animals, such as their leather, or medicines made from them (unless it is a case where life is at stake).[20]

We are forbidden from using any product derived from forbidden animals, such as their milk, eggs, fat, hair, shells, organs, bones, etc. There are significant modern implications of this, for example, the fact that we do not know which birds are *tahor* (except the three mentioned above), implies that we must consider chicken eggs and anything made with them to be tame'. Additionally, some Karaite scholars taught that the consumption of any eggs (even from a *tahor* bird) is forbidden based on the fact that the only mention of eggs in the Torah (Devarim [Deuteronomy] 22.6-7) is in the commandment that says when we find a mother bird in a nest sitting upon eggs and hatchlings that we must send away the mother bird and take the children but it does not say we may take the eggs. (See Yehudah Hadasi's Eshkol HaKofer, Alphabet 233). The glazings used to coat candies and chocolate are often derived from the secretion of the lac beetle and lac beetle shells, and are tame'. This glazing is referred to by many names, such as: Lac, Lac Resin, food glaze, or confectioner's glaze. Other waxes used to coat many fruits and vegetables are made from tame' animal fat (some of which are sold to processors under the names DK-esters and ProLong) and are referred to as food grade wax.

Rennet, an enzyme used to curdle milk to make cheese that is derived from the stomach of newborn calves, is often obtained from animals that have not been appropriately slaughtered. Therefore, one must refrain from using cheese that contains animal rennet (vegetable rennet, derived from various plant extracts or bacteria [microbial rennet], is permissible).

We are forbidden from eating any animal that has died of natural causes, or was killed by other animals – anything not properly slaughtered. (Devarim 14.21).

---

20 We are permitted to use the carcass of a normally tahor animal that has been improperly slaughtered for non-food use (i.e., as leather for shoes, belts, etc.,).

Ritual Slaughter ing and The Preparation Of Meat

A Note on the Consumption of Meat in the Diaspora:
Most of the older Karaite scholars ruled that the consumption of
meat is forbidden when we do not have the Temple (Devarim
12). Among them are: 'Anan Ben-David, Dani'el al-Qumisi, Sahl
Ben-Masli'ah, and Ya'aqov al-Qirqisani. According to 'Anan, this
prohibition did not apply to birds, or wild game, but only to
those animals which could be sacrificed. Additionally, most
prominently among the Avelei Siyyon (Mourners of Zion) and
their followers, Karaites refrained from eating meat out of
mourning for the destruction of the Temple.

In the mind of these early thinkers, the reasoning behind
the permission to eat meat was dependent on two things: the
sacrifices, and Sha'arei Yisra'el (The gates or borders of Yisra'el):
"I will spread out your border, that you may slaughter within
your gates" (Devarim 12).

Devarim 12.20-28
Because יהוה your God will enlarge your borders as
He said to you and you will say, "I would eat
meat", for it is the lust of your soul to eat meat,
you may eat meat as you wish. For if the place in
which יהוה has chosen to establish His name is too
far for you, you may slaughter any of the cattle or
herds of sheep or goats that יהוה has given you, as I
have commanded you, and eat (it) within your
gates as you wish. But as the gazelle and deer are
eaten, so may you eat it: both the person who is
tame' and the person who is *tahor* may eat it together. But make sure not to eat any blood, for the
blood is the living essence and you shall not eat
the living essence with the meat. You shall not eat
it—you shall pour it on the ground like water. You
shall not eat it, in order that it may go well for you
and for your children after you, for you will be doing that which is right in the eyes of יהוה. But your

sacred offerings and your votive offerings you shall take and come to the place which יהוה shall choose. And you shall offer your burnt offerings, both the flesh and the blood, on the altar of יהוה your God, and the blood of your slaughterings you shall pour out on the altar of יהוה your God and the meat you may eat. Keep and heed all these things which I command you in order that it may go well for you and your children after you for all eternity, for you will be doing that which is right in the eyes of יהוה.

Leading up to the 13ᵗʰ century there began to develop more lenient views, due to Rabbanite influence, where it was contended that secular slaughter was permitted anywhere outside of the land of Yisra'el . We see this, for example, in Aharon Ben-Yosef. This reasoning was based on the contention that, while the permission to eat within the borders of Yisra'el was dependent on the Temple, outside the borders of the land no such requirements obtained.

This lenience was followed by a further lenience, which said that slaughtering and eating meat is permissible anywhere outside of Yerushalayim. Aharon Ben-Eliyahu, and Eliyahu Bashyachi are examples of Hakhamim who held this position (Aderet Eliyahu, 'Inyan HaShehitah Pereq 12).

Prohibition of Blood: The main reason behind the regulations of ritual slaughter stem from the Torah's prohibition against the consumption of blood:

Bere'shit 9.4
But the flesh with its life, its blood, you shall not eat.

Wayyiqra' 7.26-27
And you shall not eat any blood in any of your habitations, whether of flying thing or beast. Anyone who eats any blood, that person shall be cut off from his people.

Devarim 12.16
Only you shall not eat the blood; you shall pour it
on the earth like water.

Regulations of Slaughter

The animals that may be eaten must be slaughtered in
accordance with Jewish law in order to be considered *tahor*.
Ritual slaughter is known as "Shehitah", and the person who
performs the slaughter is called a Shohet. Both of these words
stem from the Hebrew root Shin-Het-Tet, meaning to draw or
pull. The method of slaughter is a quick, deep drawing across the
throat with a perfectly sharp blade, severing not only the
œsophagus and trachea but both the carotid arteries and jugular
veins so that the blood may be poured out immediately as
commanded. There are a number of things that invalidate a
shehitah. The rules regulating shehitah and the preparation of
meat are as follows:

> We are prohibited from slaughtering a mother and
> its young on the same day, which implies that we
> may not slaughter a pregnant animal (Wayyiqra'
> 22.28). It is also forbidden to slaughter a newborn
> animal until after it has been able to be with its
> mother for seven days (Shemot 22.29, Wayyiqra'
> 22.27).

> All blood must be drained from the animal, and
> covered with earth (Wayyiqra' 17.13, Yehezq'el
> 24.7-8).

> Any animal slaughtered in accordance with Torah
> law, but intended for idols is forbidden (Wayyiqra'
> 17.7, Melakhim Beit [II Kings] 17.35).

After the animal has been slaughtered the meat must be porged. All its blood vessels – arteries, veins, and the smaller vessels down to the capillaries as far as this is possible – must be removed. It is especially important to remove the sinew of the veins of the sciatic nerve in the thigh muscle (Bere'shit 32.33).

Traditionally, after porging, the meat is cut into portions as required, washed well, salted, and left in a sieve for 45 minutes so that the salt can dissolve and draw out the remaining blood in the meat through osmosis. Then, the meat is rinsed three times until it is seen that the water is clear and free of blood. If the meat is intended for boiling, it is placed in boiling water and while it is cooking the froth is skimmed off. If it is placed in cold water, the blood will solidify inside the meat and this may make it unfit for eating.

If the meat is intended to be roasted, the blood that has not been drawn out in the salting is partially burnt during the roasting of the fire itself and partially trickles down and runs out. This liquid, which is a mixture of blood and fat, may not be eaten.

Traditionally, Karaites have held that fish must be killed by gathering from the water (i.e., netting them so they die from exposure to the air). This is something we learn from the Torah (BeMidbar 11.22). This is a somewhat controversial opinion.

Forbidden Fats and Nerves:

> Wayyiqra' 3.17
> [This shall be] a perpetual statute throughout your generations in all your settlements: You shall not eat any Helev nor any blood.

The Torah prohibits helev, which is a white, solid fat (as opposed to the brown fat found in tissue). There are many halavim that are forbidden: The peritoneal fat (the fat the covers the abdomen), the fat of the chest area, the fat that covers the kidneys, the kidneys themselves, the fat lobe of the liver, and the fat tail of the sheep ('alyah). The fat around the muscles is permissible. Aside from fats, the sciatic nerve and its adjoining blood vessels are also prohibited (Be'reshit [Genesis] 32.32).

Tum'ah And *Tahorah* Of Pots, Pans, Plates, Cups, Flatware, Etc.

Any utensil, or vessel that becomes tame' may not be used with or for food until it has been made *tahor*. Tame' objects can be purified in two ways:

> Cleansed by scrubbing with sweet water (Wayyiqra' 6.28, 11.32).

> Cleansed by scrubbing with sweet water and firing (BeMidbar 31.32).

Those items that cannot be purified must be destroyed, depending on the material (Wayyiqra' 11.32-35; BeMidbar 31.21-23).

Objects that become tame' are classified into three kinds:

> Vegetable matter

Clay

Stone or metal

Vegetable matter includes clothing, bed-linen, table-cloths, and wooden vessels and utensils; all these are purified by washing:

> Wayyiqra' 11.32
> And anything on which one of them falls when dead shall be tame': be it any article of wood, or clothing, or skin, or a sack – any such article that can be put to use shall be washed in water, and [it shall remain] tame' until evening; then it shall become *tahor*.

This washing is not mere rinsing but a thorough cleansing to remove every trace of that which makes the vessel tame' if any stains remain and cannot come out the item can never become *tahor* (Wayyiqra' 6.28).

Clay objects include earthenware and ceramics. These absorb the *Tum'ah* and can never be made *tahor*:

> Wayyiqra' 11.33
> And if any of those falls into an earthen vessel, everything inside it shall be tame' and [the vessel] itself you shall break.

However, glassware, such as glass cups and plates do not absorb the *Tum'ah* and therefore may be made *tahor* by washing in water. But if they are cracked they can never be made *tahor* because it is impossible to remove every trace of what made it tame' from within the cracks.

Metal or stone objects are made of gold, silver, copper, iron, steel, etc.; they may be jewelry as well as pots, pans, plates, platters, cups, goblets, flatware, etc.; if these have become tame' they must be thoroughly washed and then passed through fire to be made *tahor*. Objects made of metals that would be destroyed by fire (such as thin tin, lead, or aluminum), however, are made *tahor* by washing in water and not passed through fire:

> BeMidbar 31.23
> All articles that can withstand fire – these you shall pass through fire and to become *tahor*, but also must be cleansed with *Mei Niddah* [water of lustration][21]; and anything that cannot withstand fire you must pass through water.

In summary: Pottery objects that have become tame' must be broken, for they cannot be made *tahor*. Even the shards are tame'; but clothes and garments of various kinds, table linens, etc., as well as wooden and glass vessels and utensils may be made *tahor* by washing in water. Metal objects must, after thorough washing, be made *tahor* by fire, although objects made of metals that would be destroyed by fire must be made *tahor* by washing in water. The time at which the cleansed object becomes *tahor* is the evening following its cleansing, but it should be washed (or washed and fired, as applicable) as soon as possible after it becomes tame' and set aside until the following evening.

On Eating Out *Kasher*

Obviously, eating out in a restaurant that does not follow the laws of animal *Tum'ah* and *tahorah* is forbidden. However, one might be led to believe that eating out in a Rabbanite "*Kosher*" restaurant is acceptable. There are several significant differences in the observance of the laws of *Tum'ah* and *tahorah* between Rabbanite and Karaite Jews. Some of these differences are as follows:

---

21 See the entry on *Mei Niddah* [water of lustration] later in this chapter.

Rabbanite law regards foods that have been dried out not as food, but as wood. Since they do not consider wood to be food, anything that has been sufficiently dried to become wood, under their legal system, regardless of what it is, is considered permissible. For example, the Rabbanites permit the consumption of Pork collagen in the form of gelatin. The collagen is dried to the extent that they consider it wood, and therefore not food Yore Deah (87:10), Igros Moshe (vol:1 #37).

Rabbanite law has invented the lenience of Bittul BeShishim [nullification in sixty]: if the amount of a tame' substance is less than one part to sixty parts of food that would ordinarily be *tahor* (i.e., 1/61 of the total), then they consider the food *Kasher*. According to them this allows food to remain *tahor* after it has come in contact with a tame' substance. This is a direct violation of Wayyiqra' 11.32-40.

Rabbanite law permits the consumption of the 'Alyah [fat tail of sheep], one of the Halavim.

From this it becomes apparent that eating out in a Rabbanite "*Kosher*" restaurant is fraught with potential problems, and would, therefore, be prohibited, in general.

Human *Tum'ah* And *Tahorah*

There are a few general rules regarding human *Tum'ah* and *tahorah*:

Most cases of *Tum'ah* can be resolved by washing in sweet water before sunset. At sunset, he who was tame' and washed before sunset becomes *tahor*.

If someone who is tame' is prevented from washing prior to sunset, they will remain tame' until they are able to make themselves *tahor*.

It is forbidden for someone who is tame' to willfully fail to wash prior to sunset and thus prevent his/her becoming *tahor* at sunset, when he/she is able to do so (Wayyiqra' 5).

There are two levels of *Tum'ah*: being simply tame', and being me-tame'. Someone who has simple *Tum'ah* does not make things tame'; however, one who is metame' can make things tame'.

Shikhvat Zera' (Seminal emission)

Wayyiqra' 15.16 - 18
When a man has an emission of semen (*Shikhvat Zera'*), he shall bathe his whole body in water and [remain] tame' until evening. And any article of clothing, and any skin[22] on which there would be a spilling of semen shall be washed in water and be tame' until evening. And when man has intercourse with a woman, they shall wash with water, and they shall be tame' until evening.

Shikhvat Zera' literally means pouring out semen, i.e., seminal emission, and includes any emission of semen whether voluntary or involuntary (i.e., sexual intercourse, seminal emission due to arousal, etc.). This form of *Tum'ah* is minor, and is not communicated to any other thing that the man has ridden upon, or sat upon, or touched. Only items that have come into direct contact with the semen become tame'. The emitter himself

---

22 Skin here refers to tahor animal pelts that were used for bedding.

must bathe his whole body in sweet water, and he will remain tame' until the evening.

Miqreh Lailah (Nocturnal emission)

The man who has a nocturnal emission ("wet dream", an involuntary emission of semen that occurs when aroused while dreaming) must wash his whole body in sweet water in the latter part of the afternoon towards evening (as opposed to other forms of *Tum'ah*, where the emitter may wash any time before sunset).

Zav (Spermatorrhea, Prostatorrhea, and Urethrorrhea)

> Wayyiqra' 15.1-3
> And יהוה spoke to Mosheh and Aharon [Aaron], saying: "Speak to the Children of Yisra'el and say to them: 'Any man if he has a discharge issuing from his member, his discharge is tame'. And this shall be his *Tum'ah* in his having a discharge – whether his member flows with his discharge or is stopped up by his discharge, his *Tum'ah* is this:...

This condition is a discharge from the man's genitals in the form of semen or a semen-like fluid [i.e., mucus or pus] which issues involuntarily so that the fluid drips involuntarily from the organ in the same way as spittle drips from an animal's mouth or it coagulates and blocks the urinary tract, so that he cannot urinate, or ejaculate. All the rules of *Tum'ah* apply to such a man the whole time he has the discharge and from the day the discharge ceases he must count seven full days, and he must make himself *tahor* on the eighth day. Following are the general regulations regarding a *Zav* as dictated in Devarim 15.1-15.

> Any utensil (Hebrew keli[23]) a *Zav* sits or lies on will be metame'.

---

23 A keli is something that is literally a utensil, but refers to anything portable

Anything that comes in contact with the discharge of the *Zav* will become tame'.

Anyone who comes in contact with the keli made metame' by a *Zav* will become tame'.

Anyone who touches the *Zav* shall become tame'.

If a *Zav* spits on a person, he/she becomes tame'.

Anything that the *Zav* rides becomes tame'.

Anyone made tame' by a *Zav*, the saliva of a *Zav*, or a keli made metame' by a *Zav*, must wash his/her body and clothing and will remain tame' until evening.

When the Temple stood, at the end of the period of *Tum'ah*, the sufferer from the discharge was required to offer a burnt offering, as well as wash his whole body in sweet water – after which he would become *tahor* at sunset. the Torah continues:

Wayyiqra' 15.14
On the eighth day he shall take two turtledoves or two doves and come before יהוה at the entrance of the Tent of Meeting and give them to the priest.

Now, in the absence of the Temple, the man is unable to bring a sacrificial offering; however, he is still obligated to do all the rest of what is commanded, namely wash his whole body in sweet water, after which he will become *tahor* at sunset.

---

and not part of the ground that is being used as a utensil. A keli can also refer to items not understood in English to be utensils, such as a tent.

Niddah (The menstrual period)

The Torah states:

Wayyiqra' 15.19-20
When a woman has a discharge, her discharge
being blood in her body, she shall remain in her
[menstrual] impurity seven days; whoever touches
her shall be tame' until evening. Anything that she
lies on at the time of her impurity shall be tame';
and anything that she sits on shall be tame'.

The menstrual period is thus a period of *Tum'ah* natural
to the woman. It occurs when she observes a flow of blood; she
senses blood in her womb or private parts, or sees it on her skin
or clothing, even if it has not flowed, she is teme'ah (the feminine
of tame'). The blood from the day on which the menstruation
begins is the that which causes her to make anything upon which
she sits or lies become metame' until the sunset of the seventh
day after they are washed.

After she washes herself of the first blood she only makes
those things metame' for one day, until sunset, after they have
been washed.

This condition continues for seven days. On the eighth
day she is made *tahorah* (the feminine of *tahor*), as stated in the
Torah; at the time for her being made *tahorah* she must wash
herself, her clothes and linen, and any item with which she was
in contact during the period of *Tum'ah* in sweet water. Women
who notice a flow of water or a thick fluid are not considered
teme'ot (the feminine plural of tame'); this occurs in young girls
and in some women.

Zavah (Menorrhagia and Metrorrhagia), and the difference between Niddah and Zavah.

The Torah states:

Wayyiqra' 15.25
When a woman has had a discharge of blood for many days, not at the time of her impurity, or when she has a discharge beyond her period of impurity, she shall be teme'ah, as though at the time of her impurity, as long as her discharge lasts.

In this explicit case *Zov* means blood flowing for some days not during menstruation (Metrorrhagia), or continuing to flow after it either continuously or intermittently (Menorrhagia); such a woman is termed *Zavah* ("issuing") and not *Niddah* ("menstrually separated" – lit. impure), because the latter is purified on the eighth day as noted, while the *Zavah* is pure only after seven full days have passed from the moment of cessation of issue: For example, if a woman notices blood on a Tuesday evening, and the flow is continuous on the Wednesday and throughout the following nine days, stopping just before Friday of the following week, she begins to count seven full days from that Friday, that is, until the next Friday evening, which is the night of the eighth day. Then she is made *tahorah* and is permitted to her husband.

However, if there was a break in the flow for one day, that is, on the eighth day from the beginning of her menstrual period she was *tahorah* and on the ninth day she noticed some blood again, this is considered part of a new menstrual period and not *Zov*, and only seven days of *Tum'ah* are counted.

When the Temple was standing it was a rule from the Torah for the woman to bring a burnt offering on the day of her *tahorah*. The sacrifice was two turtledoves or two doves/pigeons, which she brought to the priest at the Temple so that be may expiate for her:

Wayyiqra' 15.29
On the eighth day she shall take two turtledoves or two pigeons, and bring them to the priest at the entrance of the Tent of Meeting.

Now, in absence of the Temple, the woman is unable to bring a sacrificial offering; but she is still obligated to do all the rest of what is commanded. It is customary for the *Zavah* to bathe her whole body in sweet water to initiate her purity after her period of *Tum'ah* has ended.

Yoledet (the woman after childbirth)

The Torah states:

Wayyiqra' 12.1-6
And יהוה spoke to Mosheh, saying: "Speak to the Children of Yisra'el saying: 'When a woman at shall produce seed and give birth to a male, she shall be *Teme'ah* unclean seven days; she shall be *Teme'ah* as at the time of her menstrual infirmity. On the eighth day the flesh of his foreskin shall be circumcised. She shall remain in a state of blood purification for thirty-three days: she shall not touch any holy thing, nor enter the Temple until her period of purification is completed. If she gives birth to a female, she shall be *Teme'ah* two weeks as during her menstruation, and she shall remain in a state of blood purification for sixty-six days. On the completion of her period of purification, for either son or daughter, she shall bring to the priest, at the entrance of the Tent of Meeting, a year old lamb for a burnt offering, and a dove/pigeon or a turtledove for a purification offering.

The calculation is therefore that following the birth of a boy the woman is *teme'ah* for forty days, and of a girl for eighty days. All the rules of *Tum'ah* of the menstrual period apply here also.

In the days of the Temple the mother was obliged to bring a sacrifice to mark the end of the period of *Tum'ah*:

> Wayyiqra' 12.6
> On the completion of her period of purification, for either son or daughter, she shall bring to the priest, at the entrance of the Tent of Meeting, a year old lamb for a burnt offering, and a dove/pigeon or a turtledove for a purification.

Now, the practices listed above concerning menstruation are followed, in the absence of the Temple and sacrifices. The rule of childbirth through Cæsarian section is the same as that of normal childbirth in all matters.

Death (Tum'at Met, and Tum'at Ohel)

Relating to the laws concerning a dead body, which, aside from *Sara'at*, is the most serious form of *Tum'ah*, the text states:

> BeMidbar 19.16
> And in the open, anyone who touches a person who was slain in battle or who died, or human bone, or a grave, shall be seven days.

In addition to washing himself with sweet water on the first day, one must wash himself on the third day and on the seventh day, after which the *Kohen* (priest) will sprinkle on him the *Mei Niddah* (see the note below)

BeMidbar 19.19
The *tahor* person shall sprinkle it upon the *tame'* person on the third day and on the seventh day, thus making him *tahor* by the seventh day. He shall then wash his clothes and wash himself with water, and at nightfall he shall become *tahor*.

And the Torah continues:

BeMidbar 19.20
If anyone who has become *tame'* fails to make himself *tahor*, that person shall be cut off from the congregation, for he has defiled the Temple of יהוה. The *Mei Niddah* was not sprinkled on him: he is *tame'*.

Again, in the absence of the Temple, High Priest, and red heifer, we do the best we can. *Tahorah* is performed by washing one's self, as prescribed above, in sweet water. In fact, that was the purification before the imposition of the commandment of sprinkling the ashes:

Wayyiqra' 22.6
A person who touches such shall be *tame'* until evening and shall not eat of the sacred donations unless he has washed his body in water.

Our sages added: "If you cannot accomplish what you want, want what you can accomplish". From this we learn that we must uphold the Torah's commandments to the extent that it is in our power.

Haggai 2.13
And Haggai said, "If someone who is *tame'* from a corpse touches any of these, will it become *tame'*?" And the priests responded and said, "Yes".

Thus we must take extreme precautions in all matters to do with *Tum'ah*, and in particular this most serious form of *Tum'ah*.

Tum'at Ohel

The corpse is the body from which the soul has utterly departed; it causes *Tum'ah* in everything within the same tent where it is located (even if it is in a coffin) and all its contents are *tame'* for seven days.

Anyone present in or entering the place where the body is located, is *tame'* for seven days:

BeMidbar 19.14-15
This is the law: when a person dies in a tent: whoever enters the tent and whoever is in the tent shall be *tame'* seven days; and every open vessel, with no lid fastened down, shall be *tame'*.

Anyone who inserts even his hand or his head or any part of his body into the place where the corpse is located, or makes indirect contact with it by means of any object or instrument, also becomes subject to the rules applying to one who comes into direct contact or enters the tent where they body is located and is unclean for seven days.

However, *Tum'ah* lasts only one day for anyone coming into contact with the deceased's bed or his effects or clothes that were on the body but later removed.

Anyone coming into contact with one who has been in direct or indirect contact is *tame'* for one day:

BeMidbar 19.22
Whatever that *tame'* person touches shall be *tame'*; and the person who touches him shall be *tame'* until evening.

'Eliyahu Bashyachi, Aderet Eliyahu, '*Inyan Tum'ah
WeTahorah, Pereq* 20
However, scripture mentioned a tent and not a house
because at that time in the wilderness they dwelt in tents... and
we shall not make an analogy about what is obligatory concerning the sprinkling of [*Mei Niddah* on] the tent to obligate
sprinkling of [*Mei Niddah* on] a house because the tent becomes
tame' because it is a *keli* and a house does not become *tame'*
because it is not a *keli*.

Sara'at (often erroneously translated as leprosy)

In Wayyiqra' chapters 13 and 14 the Torah lays out the
laws concerning the *Tum'ah* of the plague of *Sara'at*. The plague
of *Sara'at* was a scaly fungal disease, the severest form of
Tum'ah that can affect not only people, but also clothing,
bedding, tents, and even the stones of a house (which normally
do not contract *Tum'ah*). It has often been erroneously translated as leprosy, but it has nothing at all to do with the malady
medically known as Hansen's Disease.

In humans the affliction can occur spontaneously
(Wayyiqra' 13.2–17), follow a furuncle (Wayyiqra' 13.18–23) or a
burn on the skin (Wayyiqra' 13.24–28), or develop on the head
or beard (Wayyiqra' 13.29–45). The early signs of *Sara'at* in
humans are *Se'et* [a swelling or subcutaneous nodule], *Sappahat*
[a cuticular crust or scab], and *Baheret* [a whitish-red spot]. The
crux of the matter lies in the degree of cutaneous penetration
that the disease has achieved. If it affected the epidermis, or
outermost layer of skin, and did not produce pathological
changes in the hairs, the affliction was neither regarded as
especially serious nor to be *Sara'at*. As such it might consist only
of eczema, leukoderma, psoriasis, or some allied cutaneous
disease. But if the affliction has infiltrated the dermis (corium)
and has caused hairs to split or break off and lose their color,
then *Sara'at* is to be suspected. This diagnostic principle is also
applied to disease affecting the scalp (Wayyiqra' 13.29–37)

where the affliction is spoken of as *neteq* [scabby or scaly skin eruption].

The laws governing a person suffering from *Sara'at* also involved inspection by the *Kohen* at the Temple, a period of quarantine, washing one's whole body, *Mei Niddah*, sacrifices, etc.

The Torah also gives instructions with regard to *Sara'at* of clothing, bedding, etc., and the stones of houses. (Wayyiqra' 13.47-59, 14.33-55).

As noted in Aderet Eliyahu (*'Inyan Tum'ah WeTahorah*, *Pereq* 14), *Sara'at* has not been seen since before the destruction of the Temple and all its laws involve the Temple, sacrifices, the *Kohanim* serving at the Temple, *Mei Niddah*, and the land of Yisra'el . Therefore it is not applicable to our time, and we've included it here only for the sake of completeness.

Parah Adumah (The Red Heifer) and Mei Niddah (Water of Lustration)

The Torah gives instruction about the *Parah Adumah* [red heifer] whose ashes were necessary for *Mei Niddah* [water of lustration] (BeMidbar 19.2-13). These things require *Kohanim* serving in the Temple and, due to the destruction of the Temple, we are unable to do these things at this time. As with the laws regarding *Sara'at*, we've included it here only for the sake of completeness. The water of lustration, made from the ashes of the Red Heifer, were used to cleanse someone from *Tum'at met* (see *Tum'at met* above).

Unintentional Tum'ah

Especially when living in a non-Jewish world (or even in certain Jewish communities), it is very easy to become *tame'* unknowingly. As a precaution, because of the possibility of accidental *Tum'ah*, one should simply wash one's whole body daily – preferably some time closely before sunset. Regarding unintentional *Tum'ah*, the Torah says:

Yehezq'el 36.25
I will sprinkle *tahor* water upon you, and you shall
become *tahor.* I will make you *tahor* you from all
your *tum'ot*[24] and from all your *gillulim*[25].

Yehezq'el 36.29
And I shall deliver you from all your *tum'ot*, I will
summon the grain and make it abundant, and I
will not bring famine upon you.

Contamination by Fæces

The most insignificant type of *tumah* is contamination
by fæces. This occurs when someone gets fæces on themselves
after wipes from defecation, or changing a baby's diaper. In
order to become *tahor* again all that is required is that the fæces
are washed off. If the fæces stain a garment, the garment must be
washed (to the extent that the fæces have been washed out
before it is *tahor*.

Customs And Regulations Of Human *Tum'ah*

One does not go inside the *beit kenesset* [syna-
gogue], man or woman, while *tame'/teme'ah*.

In the home, special seats are reserved for those
who are *metame'* to sit on during their *Tum'ah*. In
some households, a special room is set aside for
those who are *metame'* to dwell in during their period of *Tum'ah* (This practice stems from Wayyiqra'
5.3).

---

24 The plural of *Tum'ah*.
25 The word means both idols and dung.

When *metame'* (with a communicable form of *Tum'ah*) one should refrain from touching other people, so as not to communicate the *Tum'ah* (Wayyiqra' 5.3, 15.7, 15.19, etc.,).

One should not enter the kitchen when *metame'*, with a communicable form of *Tum'ah* (*metame*), so as not to communicate the *Tum'ah* (Wayyiqra' 7.19).

During meal, persons that are *metame'* may have a special place set aside for them, away from the communal table, where they will eat.

A husband and wife do not sleep together when either of them are *metame'*. A separate bed is set aside for the *metame'* person during this period of time (Wayyiqra' 15.23).

After a period of *Tum'ah*, one should thoroughly cleanse any item they sat or lay down on (such as a chair or bed). In many instances of *Tum'ah*, these items communicate *Tum'ah* to those who touch them until they are purified (Wayyiqra' 15.5, 15.10, 15.22-23).

For all *Tum'ah*, a person should thoroughly wash their whole body in sweet water at the appropriate time. For *Tum'ah* that requires a purification sacrifice (such as the *tum'ot* of menstruation and childbirth), it is customary to light an oil lamp in the *beit kenesset* [synagogue] after purifying one's self in thanks to יהוה.

CHAPTER 6

The Family

Ancient Yisra'el 's social structure was tribal, generating tightly structured communities. These tribes saw themselves as corporate units, bound together in such a way that their presence was felt in each individual member. The people/nation ['Am or Goy] is composed of 12 tribes [Shevatim or Mattot], each of which was composed of clans [Mishpahot], and these clans were composed of extended families [Batei Avot], which were made up of households [Batim]. The clan was, thus, a super extended family.[26] The individual was neither ignored, nor were he or she considered unit on his or her own. The family was the unit. The individual found his or her place in society through the family and its extensions.

The family was the strongest unit in the social structure. It was the life-center of the people. The family would include the father, mother, and children, even after the latter had reached maturity (Shofetim 6.15; 9.1; Shemu'el Alef 16.5). The family would also had servants (bondsmen). Avraham had 318 homeborn male servants (Bere'shit 14.14), not to mention those that were not homeborn! In Torah law, families are necessary to ensure the family livelihood, to provide for the parents in their old age, and to carry on the family identity. As a result, a large

---

26 For example: People/nation: Yisra'el
Tribe: Lewi [Levi]
Clan: 'Amrami
Extended family: Beit Aharon [House of Aaron]
Household: Beit El'azar [Household of Eleazar]
Members of the household: El'azar and his wife, his son Pinhas and his wife, and his grandson Avishu'a' the son of Pinhas.

111

family is regarded as a blessing from יהוה (Shemot 1.21; Tehillim 128.3).

Legally, children were regarded as appurtaining to, and therefore the responsibility of, the father. Accordingly, a father is compensated for an accident causing the premature birth of a child (Shemot 21.22), an unmarried daughter who is seduced (Shemot 22.16), and baseless charges about his daughter's virginity that were made by her husband (Devarim 22.13-19).

Leadership of the family was by its family head, usually the eldest male. The leader and other elders were shown respect and deference. It was the family leader's task to arrange marriages (Shemot 22.17) and to discipline the children (Shemu'el Alef 3.13). The age of the children determined their rank within the family, with the eldest son having the right of primogentiure and with it, the responsibility of acting for his father in the father's absence, and who received a double portion of the father's inheritance due to those responsibilities. Joseph's brothers, for example, were seated in order of their birth, with the eldest having the seat of honor (Bere'shit 43.33).

The functions of the extended family were to provide for its own preservation, and to maintain an atmousphere of emotional warmth and stability for rearing children. The harmony of the home was necessary to provide a stable environment for its functions. Accordingly, in the Torah a number of provisions were made to ensure this harmony and to circumvent competition that would endanger it, for example the law forbidding marriage of sisters to the same husband (Wayyiqra' 18.18), which would only create competition between the sisters. Also, there are the laws prohibiting incest, which, again, promote harmony in the household and family unit. Given a better understanding of the Ancient Hebrew family unit, it becomes more apparent why inmarriage among family members was restricted to such a wide extent.

The social foundations for the Torah's focus on responsibility and motives may be traced to its understanding that an individual cannot act in such a way that his deeds have no effect on others, whether or not those effects are visible in the present. Rather than seeing infractions as isolated incidents, a violator endangered his group by bringing guilt upon them, whether it be upon an entire people (as the Gileadite altar, Yehoshu'a' 22.19-20) or the succeeding generations (as in the sin of idolatry, Shemot 20.5; 34.7; BeMidbar 14.18; Devarim 5.9). The people convicted of adultery became a curse on the community to which they belonged (BeMidbar 5.27). Oft-cited examples are the sin of 'Akhan that brought guilt on his family and through it, to the entire people of Yisra'el (Yehoshu'a' 7.24). The families of Datan, Aviram, and Qorah, and the latter's household, were destroyed because of the rebellion of their leaders (BeMidbar 16.32-35).

Honoring Parents

As previously noted, the root of the Hebrew word for honor, *kavod*, means being substantial or weighty. To honor someone, is to give weight to or to grant a person a position of respect and even authority in one's life. The Torah tells us that we should honor our parents.

While honor is an internal attitude of respect, courtesy, and deferenece, it should be accompanied by appropriate attention or even obedience. Honor without such action is incomplete; it is lip service (Yesha'yahu 29.13). The following laws relate to honoring our parents.

We are commanded to honor our parents (Shemot 20.12)

Anyone who attacks or curses his father or his mother is subject to the death penalty (Shemot 21.15, 17; cf. Devarim 21.18-21).

The commandment to honor one's parents and hold them in awe is the fifth of the *'Aseret HaDevarim* [the "Ten pronouncements", often inaccurately referred to as "Ten

Commandments"]; fulfilling it carries its own reward, explicitly stated:

> Shemot 20.12
> Honor your father and your mother, that you may long endure on the land that יהוה your God is giving to you.

In Devarim the rewards are augmented:

> Devarim 5.16
> Honor your father and your mother, as יהוה your God has commanded you, that you may long endure, and that you may fare well, in the land that יהוה your God is giving to you.

Our sages determined two ways we honor our parents: honor in words (not speaking ill of them, speaking respectfully of them and to them) and honor in deeds – that is, material support for them. Similarly, in behavior, one should rise in their presence and go towards them (c.f. Eliyahu Bashyachi, *Aderet Eliyahu, 'Inyan Kibbud Av WaEm*).

Just as a man is obliged to respect his parents while they live, so must he respect them after their death. This is done by attending to the burial with great dignity and by placing a gravestone over the grave; by mourning them; by commemorating their memory in the *beit kenesset* for a year on every Sabbath and on all possible occasions as according to custom.

Ni'uf ["Adultery"]

Ni'uf, while commonly translated as adultery, does not have the exact same meaning as the the English word. *Ni'uf* is based upon the woman's marital status: if she is married or *mequdeshet* ["betrothed"] and has sexual relations with a man other than her husband or betrothed the act is *ni'uf*, regardless of the status of the man involved. In Babylonian, Assyrian, and Hittite laws[27] the husband had the right to prosecute or to drop charges against his wife and her paramour. The husband has no such option in Torah, nor has the state any expressed right to pardon the guilty parties. The absence of such an explicit legal rule leads one to conclude that, since prosecution in Mesopotamia was a matter of private preference, the offense was considered primarily as a violation of property rights. But in Yisra'el , where the matter is an obligation of the whole people to bring the matter before the *Shofetim* to prosecute, the matter was construed primarily as a crime against יהוה and society. These two factors—the rôle of the people in prosecution, and the death penalty awarded the guilty parties—point to criminal rather than civil law. The matter is all the clearer when Assyrian and Hittite law affords the husband the right to dispatch both guilty parties on the spot if caught in the act, whereas the executioner in Yisra'el was always the community, or its representatives. Accordingly, *ni'uf* must be seen as a crime against יהוה and the people that threatened society, and only secondarily against the husband.

Today, the punishment for *ni'uf*, is the same as that given to other sins that require the death penalty.

> Binyamin al-Nahawandi, *Ma'sat Binyamin*
> If testamony is given against a married woman that she has lain with another man, both are subject to the penatly of death... However, since we no longer inflict the punishment of death, she must instead remain forbidden to her husband, and both she and her paramour must be kept apart from the congregation...

---

27 See The Code of Hammurapi, 129 (on page 171), The Middle Assyrian Laws, 14-16 (on page 181), and The Hittite Laws, 197-198 (on page 196) in J. B. Pritchard, Ancient Near East Texts (1970).

Gilui 'Arayot ["Incest"]

Gilui 'arayot, while usually translated as incest, is much more inclusive and covers a much wider number of forbidden relationships. *gilui 'arayot*, like *ni'uf*, was punishable by death (Wayyiqra' 20.11-12,14,17,19-21). One's father's wife, mother-in-law, and sister (including one's half-sister) are declared forbidden degrees of sexual relationship in Devarim 22.30; 27.20, 22-23, to which Wayyiqra' 18.6-18 adds one's mother, granddaughter, aunt (including the wife of one's uncle), daughter-in-law, sister-in-law, one's wife's child or grandchild, and the sister of one's wife. The Torah uses the term *Kol She'er Basar* [all persons of near kinship]. The degree of kinship between a man and his aunt is the same as that between a woman and her uncle, therefore The Torah forbids a man from having sexual relations with his niece as well. That the issue is not the genetic stability of the offspring can be demonstrated by the inclusion of a number of "inlaws" who have no genetic relationship to the perpetrator.

Again, lying behind the laws against *gilui 'arayot* are the concepts of *qedushah* [holiness] and the intention to safeguard the solidarity of the family from internal sexually generated tensions. Sexual activity within the home, beside that carried on within the bonds of marriage, introduces the element of rivalry with its concomitant alienation. Those elements are hostile to the solidarity of the home that is valued so highly in the *TaNaKh* and that is so vital to a healthy and holy society. Evidence for this interpretation may be found in the laws against one's marrying two sisters (Wayyiqra' 18.18) or a mother and her daughter (Wayyiqra' 18.17). *Gilui 'arayot*, therefore, becomes criminal for the same reason as *ni'uf*: it fragments the home, and, with it, the community, the tribe, and the people.

Gender Rôles

Unfortunately, to many people the acceptability of the *TaNaKh*'s models in determining a theology of sexuality often turns, not on the validity of the models or the supporting evidence in the *TaNaKh*, but on the way in which that theology is seen through the current fashions of society. On one pole there are the male supremacists who will insist that, just as woman's creation was somewhat of a divine afterthought, so she is inherently inferior and her gender rôle must reflect that subservience to the male in all its aspects. Close to the other end are some who would insist that there is no equality without identicalness and that the woman's rôle in any society must be exactly the same as the man's in all respects.

In the Torah, men and women do have separate rôles. For example, according to Torah law, a man does have some level of authority over his wife (BeMidbar 30.13). However, from this it must not be inferred that the Torah dictates subjegation, or inferiority for women. The numerous stories of women who were heroes (Devorah, Avigayil, etc.) or villains (Izevel, 'Atalyah) clearly show that women had a degree of self-determination that modern people sometimes ignore. What the Torah shows us is a world where men and women are equal in justice and honor, and differentiated in teleology.

All in all, the Torah is very sparse in dictating differences between men and women with regard to rôles. The implication of this is that, despite a few exceptions, the Torah does not dictate gender rôles.

The Eduction And Upbringing Of Children

A community secures its continued existence and development only through the transmission of its accumulated knowledge and philosophical aims to the next generation. The *TaNaKh* repeatedly indicates that the success of our community and the continuity of our society are conditioned by our knowledge of and obedience to יהוה's revealed law (Yehoshu'a' 1.6-8). Thus, to ensure our prosperity, growth, and longevity as the people of יהוה, we are mandated to diligently teach our children love and respect of יהוה, and to know and obey His Torah (Devarim 6.1-9).

As can be imagined, Torah should constitute the central focus of a child's education. Its imprint should be felt in all areas of instruction.

Education is much more than just the teaching of mechanics, such as reading and arithmetic. The education of a young mind should be directed; it should have a goal. An education founded on the principles of Torah should have as its goal the creation of a member loyal to יהוה and Torah, family, clan, tribe, and people.

The Torah commands parents to teach their children and instruct them in the ways of the Torah, wisdom, and the commandments (Devarim 6.7, 11.19). *Hakham* Elyahu Bashyachi wrote: "This commandment holds even if the father derives no pleasure from the son..."[28], i.e., he is obligated to educate his child even if the child is lacking in respect.

The education of a child by its parent strengthens a family. It fosters a level of respect in the relationship between parent and child. It creates a link that transcends generations, and brings new depth and importance to what might otherwise be deemed routine work. Education passed down from generation to generation has a history and context no other form of education could ever possibly attain. In fact, until quite recently, the majority of the education a child received came from his parents.

While the *TaNaKh* emphasizes the rôle of the father as teacher, both parents are required to train their children (Mishlei 1.8, 6.20; 31.26).

The family (extended family) and the religious community also play an important rôle in the education of children. Community instruction takes the form of didactic and historical study, moral training, sign and symbol memorization, festival and sacrificial liturgy, ritual enactment, and priestly rôle modeling. Specific examples of community education include: the three great pilgrimage festivals *Hagh HaMassot, Hagh*

---

28 Sefer Aderet Eliyahu, Seder 'Inyan HaTefillah, Heleq Rishon, 'Iqqqarei HaEmunah, Ha'Iqqar HaShishi (page 167 in the 1966 Ramlah reprint of the 1870 Odessa edition).

HaShavu'ot, and *Hagh HaSukkot* (Devrarim 16.16; cf. Shemot 12.14-28), the public reading of the Mosaic law every seventh year (Devarim 31.12-13), the covenantal renewal enactments (Devarim 29-30; Yehoshu'a' 23-24), the annual national festivals and fasts, *Shabbat* worship, historical teaching memorials, Tabernacle/Temple architecture and furnishings, the sacrificial system, and priestly dress and liturgical function.

A few other specific characteristics of Torah education that stand out are:

> Torah education stresses the importance of recognizing and remembering events of divine providence in history as living elements of modern life.

> The idea of indeterminism or personal freedom in the *TaNaKh* gives people dignity as free moral agents in creation; likewise a Torah education stresses the responsibility individuals have toward יהוה and others, accountability of human behavior, and the need for disciplined training in making right choices.

> The notion in the Torah that we are divinely chosen closely binds us to the Jewish people; and this relationship takes a significant rôle in Jewish education. We are obligated to live up to the demands of יהוה's holiness in order to remain his special possession, while educationally we are obligated to instruct all nations in divine holiness as יהוה's instrument of light to the nations.

A Torah based education is both objective (external and content oriented) and subjective (internal and personally oriented), cognitive (emphasis on the intellect) and affective (emphasis on the will and emotions), and both active (investigative and participatory) and passive (routine and reflective). Just as the Torah affects all aspects of life, so an education founded on Torah should impact all aspects of a person.

Torah education encompasses the unique covenantal history of a people chosen by יהוה. A focus of the education is the particular content of the series of covenantal agreements or treaties יהוה made with us. These covenants form the basis of our relationship to תיהוה and are characterized by the inclusion of legislation and stipulations necessary for maintaining that relationship.

Mosheh summarized the basic goals of Jewish education in his farewell address as loving יהוה, walking in His ways, and keeping His commandments, statutes, and ordinances (Devarim 30.16).

The practice of education as outlined in the Torah results in יהוה's blessing. These divine blessings include political auton-omy and security, and agricultural and œconomic prosperity (Wayyiqra' 26.1-8). Sociologically, the practice of education facilitates assimilation into the community of Yisra'el ; and it ensures the stabilization of that community (Wayyiqra' 19.15,18). Religiously, the practice of education sustains our covenantal relationship with יהוה through obedience and service, which prompt יהוה's favor and presence (though they do not determine it).

Relations Of Husband And Wife

Leadership of the family, historically, has been the responsibility of the eldest male in a household. However, it is important to keep in mind that the Torah, while it does delegate specific authority to a husband[29], does not dictate that a husband is the ruler of a household. As the Torah depicts them, wives have much more power than they are often credited with. Sarah, for example, after urging Avraham to have sexual relations with her maidservant Hagar in order to father a child, expels both

---

29 For more information, see the section on oaths.

Hagar and her teenaged son over the protests of Avraham; and יהוה tells Avraham to listen to Sarah (Bere'shit 21.9-13). The functions of the extended family provide for its perpetuation and maintain an atmousphere of emotional warmth and stability for rearing children. The harmony of the home is vitally necessary to provide a stable environment for its functions. Accordingly, the Torah dictates a number of provisions to ensure this harmony and to circumvent rivalries that would endanger it and cause the home to break apart. For example, the law forbidding marriage of sisters to the same husband (Wayyiqra' 18.18), is an obvious effort to avoid the sort of strife that had infected Ya'aqov 's household. Also, the commandment guaranteeing the rights of children that cannot be supplanted by favoritism to another child (Devarim 21.15-17).

Abortion

Conception and childbirth are gifts from יהוה. The often misunderstood Bere'shit 1.28, "be fruitful and multiply...", is less a set of divinely imposed obligations to populate and to rule, than it is a revelation of God-given blessings. This manifestation of divine blessing in the form of posterity is echoed in יהוה's judgment on the serpent (Bere'shit 3.15), and continues as the heart of יהוה's commitments to Avraham (Bere'shit 17.6, 16; 21.1-2), Yishaq (26.3-4, 24), Ya'aqov (28.14; 30.18, 20; 33.5) and all Yisra'el (Devarim 7.13); as the reward to Shifrah and Pu'ah, two midwives, for their refusal to commit infanticide (Shemot 1.20-21); and as an assurance to wives who, being falsely accused of unfaithfulness, pass the ritual test for defilement (BeMidbar 5.28). The restoration of Iyyov is marked by the blessing of offspring (Iyyov 42.12-17); and The Psalmist depicts the blessing, particularly of sons, in terms of inheritance and divine reward, legal protection, and prestige (Tehillim 127.3-5; cf. 113.9; 128.3-4). In our own age, characterized as it is by a perceived overpopulation, birth control, and increasingly fragmented families, the Biblical portrait of the child as divine blessing may appear quaint to some, and even oppressive to others.

Nevertheless, it would be unwise to dismiss outright so consistent a testimony. Pregnancy is never seen as a curse, nor children as divine punishment for sexual promiscuity. The contrary is, in fact, true.

A second, related theme, most prominent once again in the narratives of Bere'shit, portrays יהוה directly involved in both causing and preventing fertility. More than once, יהוה's merciful intervention stands out against a backdrop of barrenness and despair. Most striking are the accounts of the three matriarchs, Sarah, Rivqah, and Rahel, each of whom saw barrenness give way to fruitfulness as יהוה set out to fulfill his promise to Avraham. Sometimes, יהוה's intervention is noted in passing, without explanation (Bere'shit 4.1; Rut 4.13), but other times יהוה's bestowal of fertility or infertility is in direct response to obedience or disobedience (Shemot 23.26; Wayyiqra' 20.20-21; Devarim 7.13-14; 30.5, 30.9; Hoshe'a' 9.11). Biblical evidence stops short of suggesting that every conception is a direct act of divine causation; neither is barrenness infallibly linked with divine displeasure. Nevertheless יהוה's initiative, causing or preventing conception or stillbirth, surely establishes this domain as one in which יהוה is intensely interested and over which יהוה is ultimately sovereign.

Given the silence of the *TaNaKh* on the issue, one can assume that for the Jewish family, the intentional termination of pregnancy (abortion) was unknown, distasteful, or even unconscionable. Clearly, many elements of the Mosaic code directly targeted Yisra'el 's inclination to adopt immoral practices deeply ingrained in Cana'anite practice, including the abhorrent ritual of child sacrifice. Thus, while Torah law addressed explicitly offensive cultic practices that posed an obvious threat, abortion was not directly mentioned.

Within the body of Torah legislation, the most explicit discussion of the unborn child occurs in Shemot 21.22-25, which describes a premature delivery caused by a push or blow, almost certainly accidental, to a pregnant woman. The gap between this scenario and an act of premeditated abortion is a wide one, but it does provide important clues regarding the nature and extent of

יהוה's concern for a fœtus. The crucial phrase, *weyas'u yeladeiha* (lit. "and her children come out"), is necessarily interpretive. Although the verb *yasa'* (go out, come out, come forth) routinely describes normal, live birth[30], it may on occasion refer to stillbirth (Shemot 21.22). The flexibility of the term allows for both. Generally, though, when the text wants to speak of bereavement, it uses the word *nefel* – which is absent in this passage.

Verse 22, however, provides further clarification. It stipulates: "*im lo' yihyeh ason*" [if no catastrophe occurs], then the perpetrater is only fined and the husband paid compensation for the premature birth (which usually meant greater convalescence for the mother and an endangerment to the stregnth and health of the child), but in verses 23-25 it says "*Weim-ason yihyeh wenatatah nefesh tahat nefesh. 'ayin tahat 'ayin shen tahat shen yad tahat yad reghel tahat reghel. Kewiyyah tahat kewiyyah pesa' tahat pesa' habburah tahat habburah*" [And if there occurs a catastrophe you shall exact the penalty life for life, eye for eye, tooth for tooth, hand/arm for hand/arm, foot/leg for foot/leg, burn for burn, wound for wound, bruise for bruise] referring to harm suffered by mother or child, ranging from minor trauma to death. In this case, fœtal and maternal death are treated equally, implying that fœtus and mother have the same legal status. The opposition in the text is between premature delivery and harm. Moreover, the author would have added "*lah*" ["to her"] if the harm in view was only to the mother. Torah thus establishes that causing the death of the fœtus, even accidentally, is morally culpable. Plainly, no authority to perform abortion is granted (except when the life of the mother is imperiled).

Birth Control

The Torah does not deal with the issue of birth control, *per se*. The use of birth control, therefore, aside from the use of

---

30 (Bere'shit 25:25-26; 38:28-30; Iyyov 1:21; 3:11; Qohelet 5:15; Yirmiyahu 1:5;

abortion as birth control, is up to the discretion of each individual. However, one must remember that the ingestion of hormones from *tame'* animals is forbidden, just as is the ingestion of any other part of a *tame'* animal.

20:18; cf. Devarim 28:57; Iyyov 38:8, 29).

CHAPTER 7

Prayer and the Synagogue

A synagogue, and its surrounding structures, is the modern center of Jewish religious life. In Karaite life, the sole function of the synagogue, or *beit kenesset* (literally house of assembly), is a place of prayer and religious study. Jews can satisfy the obligations of daily prayer by praying in almost any *tahor* place that is devoid of images; however, being that the obligatory prayer is not a personal matter, but a communal responsibility, it is better to pray together with the community in a place dedicated to it. The sanctity of the Karaite *beit kenesset* for this purpose is modeled on the *Beit HaMiqdash* [Temple]. Often attached to the Karaite synagogue are houses of study, and community halls (for gatherings such as marriages, *Berit Milah* [ritual circumcision] ceremonies, and other communal events). If there is no study hall attached to the synagogue, study is performed in the sanctuary itself.

Batei kenesset (the plural of *beit kenesset*) are generally run by a board of directors composed of lay people. They manage and maintain the *beit kenesset* and its activities. It is worth noting that a synagogue can exist without a *Hakham*: prayer services are conducted by lay people in whole or in part. However, the *Hakham* is a valuable member of the community, providing leadership, guidance and education.

Synagogues, and the communal structures attached to them, are financed through membership dues paid annually, and through voluntary donations. It is important to note, however, that one does not have to be a member of a *beit kenesset* in order to worship there. If one plans to worship at a synagogue

125

regularly, and has the financial means, they should certainly pay their dues to cover their share of the synagogue's costs, but no Karaite *beit kenesset* checks membership cards at the door.

The portion of the *beit kenesset* where *tefilah* [prayer] is performed is commonly called the sanctuary. Synagogues in the United States are generally designed so that the front of the sanctuary is on the side towards Yerushalayim, which is the direction that we are supposed to face when reciting prayers.

Probably the most important feature of the sanctuary is the Ark, or *Aron* in Hebrew. The Ark is a cabinet or recession in the wall that holds the Torah scrolls. It is always placed on the wall facing Yerushalayim, the direction of Prayer. The Ark often (but not always) has doors as well as a *parokhet* [curtain, from the root *Pe'-Resh-Kaf*, to shut off] (which most often is in front of the doors, if there are any, and sometimes inside behind the doors). This curtain is in imitation of the dividing curtain in the Sanctuary in the Temple. Prior to the reading of the *Sefer Torah*, the doors (if there are any) and curtain of the Ark are opened, so that the *Sefer Torah* may be taken out.

In addition, you may find a *menorah* [literally, a seven branched lamp-stand for oil lamps, but today also applied to a candelabrum] or even several *menorot* in many synagogues as a reminder of the *menorah* in the Temple. The *menorah* in the synagogue will generally have seven branches, but six branched *menorot* may also be found. The *menorot* in a *beit keneset* will not have the same dimensions or decorative features as the Temple *menorah*, because exact duplication of the Temple's ritual items is forbidden by Torah.

The *Aron* is located on a *bimah* [raised platform]. On the *bimah*, in front of the *Aron*, is the *tevah* [the large reading table, literally box] on which the *Sefer Torah* is placed when it is read. The *tevah* is also used as a lectern for leading services on *Shabbatot* [Sabbaths] and *mo'adim* [holidays, literally "appointed times"]. There is also an additional one to three lower smaller *tevot* [lecterns] on the main floor of synagogue, one of which is used as the lectern for leading weekday services.

Synagogues have separate seating sections for women. This is usually just the area of the room behind the men; however, in some synagogues, that have a large attendance and cannot accommodate everyone on one floor, it may be on an upper floor balcony, or, rarely, on the side of the room. Women and Men in a Karaite synagogue are separated during prayer solely for reasons of modesty. The need for these measures to preserve modesty stems from *hishtahawayah* [bowing down], which occurs during prayer (see the section on prayer for more detail). Quite simply, a woman bowing in front of a man could easily expose herself.

Non-Jews Visiting A Synagogue

We always welcome non-Jews who come to synagogue out of genuine curiosity, interest in the service, or simply to join a friend in celebration of a Jewish event.

In general a non-Jew should follow the same dress and behavior requirements followed by the Jews who are attending services. Non-Jews should not, however, wear a *Tallit* (prayer shawl).

During services, non-Jews can follow along silently in the prayers with the English translation, which might be printed side-by-side with the Hebrew in the *siddur* [prayerbook]. They may join in with as much or as little of the prayer service as they feel comfortable participating in. A review the liturgy before attending the service, will provide the non-Jew a better understanding of what is going on.

A special note about preparations: Non-Jews visiting a Karaite *beit kenesset* should contact a *Hakham* prior to attending in order to discuss with him or her how to prepare themselves to enter the synagogue. A Karaite *beit kenesset* is *tahor* [ritually pure] and, consequently, everyone who attends must also be *tahor*. A non-Jew should never attend a Karaite *beit kenesset* without first ensuring they are appropriately prepared.

Behavior In The Synagogue

Due to its holy purpose as a house of prayer and religious study, one must respect the *beit kenesset* as such and not carry on personal conversations, business transactions, joking, or gaming during services. One should maintain its cleanliness and *tahorah* [ritual purity], not eat or drink in it, and not bring into it any foul thing.

Synagogue Personnel

The Hakham

The *Hakham* is primarily a religious teacher who oversees the instruction of the community and answers questions on the understanding of the *TaNaKh* and points of *Halakhah*.

The Ba'al Qeri'ah

It is normally the responsibility of each congregant called to the Torah to read the Torah himself, however, when the congregants are not knowledgeable enough to do the reading, a *Ba'al Qeri'ah* [literally a "master of the reading"] may be designated to do the reading for the congregants.

The Gabbai

The *Gabbai* is the treasurer for the synagogue and is responsible for the disbursement of funds for the upkeep and repair of the synagogue.

The Shammash

The *Shammash* is the custodian of the synagogue and is responsible for its upkeep.

The Hazzan

The *Hazzan* is the person who leads prayer. Any member of the congregation who is knowledgeable enough may act as *Hazzan*. At times, when there is no one else able to perform this function, the *Hakham* will also act as *Hazzan*.

The Worship Services

Tefillah [Prayer]

While the mandatory public prayer, performed at sunset and sunrise, comes overwhelmingly from the text of the *TaNaKh*, voluntary private prayer can be said anytime, can be anything that comes from the heart of the individual, and may be offered in any *tahor* place.

For the Karaite prayer is many things. It is, first of all, an obligation. As a temporary replacement for the sacrifices of the *Beit HaMiqdash* [Temple] (until that time when it will be rebuilt), we are required to offer our sacrifices of prayer twice daily, just as the sacrifices were offered twice daily in the Temple (see Hoshe'a' 14.3). Prayer is also, concomitantly, a means of communicating with יהוה, and a way of understanding our relationship to יהוה as individuals and a community.

History of Prayer in Karaism

The Karaite prayer book (Siddur) we have today is a late text that comes to us from the Byzantine community. It was redacted in the thirteenth century by Aharon Ben-Yosef (called Aharon HaRishon [the former] to distinguish him from Aharon Ben-Eliyahu (who is referred to as Aharon HaSheni [the second]). While it contains mostly elements of the older Karaite liturgy from the Yerushalayim community it also has numerous additions (including piyyutim [liturgical poems] from later Byzantine, Crimean, Galician, Wolhynian, and Lithuanian Karaites, as well as from the Andalusian Rabbanites who so significantly influenced the Byzantine Karaites).

Karaites have always relied on the TaNaKh to provide material for prayer. The Karaites of the Yerushalayim school relied heavily on the books of Tehillim and Eikhah in the composition of their liturgy; however, they felt free to use passages from any place in scripture to provide them with the words they felt best expressed what they were attempting to communicate.

Prayer in the ancient communities was much less structured than it is today. This is not to say that there were not basic principles that guided prayer, but there was a general tendency to avoid its canonization. According to Yefet Ben-'Eli HaLewi (a prominent figure during this time), there are twelve elements that are mandatory in prayer[31]:

1. Mentioning the creation and its arrangement.

2. Mentioning יהוה's excellences and His general and particular beneficence.

3. Mentioning the wonders, miracles, and signs performed by יהוה in the past and those He will perform in the future.

4. The disobedience of our ancestors.

5. The punishment which overtook them.

6. The return of the repentant.

---

31 See his commentary on Tehillim: "It is obligatory for us to include these twelve themes in our mandatory prayers, day and night".

7. Their (the repentants') request to יהוה for knowledge of His Scripture.

8. Their (the repentants') request for salvation from their enemies.

9. Their (the repentants') request that יהוה fulfill His promises to redeem them.

10. The conversion of the gentile nations to the true belief in יהוה, the one and only God, and their eternal thanks to יהוה.

11. Recounting universal and perpetual peace and banishment of enmity among the nations.

12. The obedience of the nations to יהוה's people and His Mashi'ah (Messiah, i.e., the reinstated House of Dawid [David] as the anointed kings of Yisra'el).

As Karaism evolved, the relationship of the movement to prayer changed. With the coming of the prayer book, the method of communal prayer was formalized. Fixed formulæ of blessings, like those of the Rabbanites arose undoubtedly through Rabbanite influence. In general, with a few noted exceptions, Karaite prayer has continued to be based almost solely on scripture.

Modern Prayer

Before entering the house of prayer, one must remove his or her shoes, wash one's hands and cover one's head. The reason for this is that we consider the house of prayer like a "little sanctuary [*Miqdash Me'at*]".

Yehezq'el 11.16
Therefore say: "Thus said the Lord יהוה: 'Because I have removed them far among the nations and have scattered them among the countries, and I have become to them a little sanctuary in the countries where they have gone.'"

Many of the practices we observe in the synagogue derive from the custom of treating the synagogue like the Temple [*Miqdash*] (in all ways this is appropriate).

The prayer service always begins with the worshipper putting on the *Tallit* [prayer shawl]. This action is predeced by the following blessing:

Barukh Atah יהוה Eloheinu Melekh Ha'Olam Asher Qiddeshanu BeMiswotaiw WeSiwwanu LiLbosh Arba' Kanfot Ba*Sisit*: Amen.

Blessed are you, יהוה our God, Ruler of the universe who has sanctified us with his commandments and commanded us to wear four cornered garments with the *sisit*. Amen.

The *Tallit* is then placed over the shoulders, and around the back, like a normal cloak cloak, but is sometimes folded into a relatively narrow band and worn draped across the shoulders and down the front of the body like a stole. The *Tallit* is worn throughout the service. If at any time one needs to leave the sanctuary, for example to releive oneself, the *Tallit* should be removed and left in the sanctuary. It may be put on again, without the blessing, when returning to the services.

The services are always initiated by the *Hazzan* (the person designated to lead the servies). During the course of the service, the *Hazzan* and the congregation exchange the reading of the prayers. In technical terms, this is called antiphony. This is to say that the service is conducted in a dialogue between the *Hazzan* and the congregation. The *Hazzan* will read a line, or a portion of a line, and the congregation will respond by reading the next line, or finishing the line the *Hazzan* began.

Each section of the prayer has a specific melody assigned to it; and the best way for someone to learn these melodies is to regularly attend services.

Customarilly, there are positions assumed during prayer; these are included in every service, whether the prayer is uttered alone or with a congregation, whether the service is for *Shabbat*, a *Mo'ed*, a *Hagh*, or for an ordinary weekday. They are as follows:

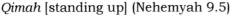

Qimah [standing up] (Nehemyah 9.5)

Hishtahawayah [bowing down] (Tehillim 5.8)

Keri'ah and *Berikhah* [kneeling down and standing upon the knees] (Tehillim 95.6)

Nefilat Apayim [falling on the face] (Bere'shit 17.3)

Nesi'at 'Einayim [lifting up the eyes] (Tehillim 123.1)

Perisat Yadayim [stretching forth the hands] (Tehillim 143.6)

Hizdaqfut [standing up straight] (Tehillim 145.14, 146.8)

Nesi'at Yadayim [lifting the hands] (Tehillim 28.2)

Se'aqah and *Qeri'ah* [crying out and calling out] (Eikhah 3.55, Tehillim 34.18)

Other elements that should be present when we pray are an active sense of awe for יהוה, and moments of silent, internal prayer.

Behavior During Services

Beyond the positions and provisions of prayer there are general expectations for behavior during services that every worshipper should try to follow. In general, these are simply a matter of respect and consideration:

Arrival at the synagogue in time for the start of the service.

Donning the *Tallit*.

Following the *Hazzan* during the calling out, the standing, the bowing down, and the kneeling – attempting to keep up with the congregation.

Keeping silent and refraining from talking during the service, the reading of the Torah, the memorials, and the blessings.

Refraining from accompanying out loud the reading by the *Hazzan* or other reader who is leading the service at that time.

Responding at the pauses in or at the end of the reading of his part by the *Hazzan* or by any other person who has been given the honor of reading.

Responding in unison with the congregation.

Refraining from lazy pronunciation. An attempt should be made to read the text clearly, and understand it, not just mimic the sounds of the words. Along these lines, responses to the *Hazzan* should be withheld until a pause in the passage or until the end of the verse, so as not to muddle the words of prayer.

The prayer must be conducted with complete attention, with great reverence, and with no changes in the intonation.

As with the prayer of the ancient Karaim, so we too have specific elements that must be addressed in every prayer service. There are seven. They are:

1.   *Berakhah* [Blessing]

The hymns "May the name of יהוה be blessed, etc".(Tehillim 113, etc.), from the Morning Service, and "I will bless יהוה at all times" (Tehillim 34.2 etc.) from the Evening Service.

2.   *Shevah* [Praise]

Tehillim 117.1
Praise יהוה, all nations; extol Him, you peoples.

The hymns for each day, all of which constitute praise for יהוה; and also:

Tehillim 145.4
One generation to another shall laud Your works to another and tell of Your mighty acts.

3.   *Romemut* [Exalting]

Tehillim 145.1
I will extol You, my God, the King; And I will bless Your name forever and ever.

4.   *Hoda'ah* [Acknowledgment]

This is in the statement: "Hear O Yisra'el , יהוה our God יהוה is One". (Devarim 6.4), and in the statement: "One is our God; great is יהוה; holy and awe inspiring is his name for ever and ever".

5.   *Widui* [Confession]

From the sentence, "And now what shall we say, our God", ('Ezra 9.10, etc.). Also: "Our God and God of our fathers we have sinned, etc". (from the *Shabbat* Morning Service after reading the passage about the *Shabbat* sacrifices), which is a confession of our sins.

6.   *Baqashah* [Entreaty]

The entreaty always follows the confession; in it the worshipper asks for forgiveness and absolution for transgression, for example:

Dani'el 9.19
"O Lord, hear! O Lord, forgive! O Lord, listen, and act, do not delay, for Your own sake, O my God; for Your name is called upon Your city and Your people!"

7.   *Tehinah* [Supplication]

This is included in the entreaty:

Dani'el 9.18
Incline Your ear, O my God, and hear; open Your eyes and see our desolation and the city upon which Your name is called. For not because of any merit of ours do we lay our plea before You but because of Your abundant mercies.

These seven elements are all included in the prayer "*Barukh Shimkha*" [Blessed is your name], which is recited in unison at the end of every service by the entire congregation. When they are read out, each worshipper bows their head (from the waist) as a sign of reverence.

Finally, there are five specific *qeddushot* [sanctifications] called out during the service that are of specific importance. Each one corresponds to one of the books of the Torah. When they are read out, each worshipper bows their head (from the waist) as a sign of reverence.

1.   The first sanctification (representing Bere'shit):

Tehillim 22.4
And You are Holy, who is enthroned on the praises of Yisra'el .

This recalls the basis of the book, since in Bere'shit we are made aware of יהוה's existence through the creation of the universe.

2.   The second sanctification (representing Shemot):

Yesha'yahu 47.4
"Our Reedemer, יהוה of hosts is his name, the Holy One of Yisra'el ".

This recalls the second book, which is the story of the redemption from Egypt of Yisra'el , whom He saved from the hand of their enemy.

3.   The third sanctification (representing Wayyiqra'):

Yesha'yahu 6.3
And one would call to the other,
"Holy, holy, holy!
יהוה of Hosts!
The fullness of the earth is His Glory!"

This recalls the third book, in which יהוה gave us the laws of holiness, sanctifying Yisra'el from all other nations in the matters of the sacrifices, *Niddah*, *Sara'at*, incestuous relationships, etc. that separates the nation of Yisra'el from the rest of the nations.

4. The fourth sanctification (representing BeMidbar):

Yehezq'el 3.12
"Blessed is the Glory of יהוה from His place".

This recalls the fourth book, which details the orders of the Tabernacle and the of the cloud that provided us with guidance in the desert and descended upon the Tabernacle in glory (see BeMidbar 9.15-10.36).

5. The fifth sanctification is (representing Devarim):

Devarim 6.1
"Hear O Yisra'el , יהוה our God יהוה is One".

This recalls the last book, in which this verse is found. It is to remind us that, despite the many attributes of the Creator, such as Redeemer, Holy, etc., יהוה is One.

Berakhot [Blessings]

Blessings for Food and Drink

Devarim 6.10-12
So it shall be, when יהוה your God brings you into
the land of which He swore to your fathers, to
Avraham, to Yishaq, and to Ya'aqov, to give you
large and beautiful cities which you did not build,
and houses full of all good things which you did
not fill, and hewn-out cisterns which you did not
hew, and vineyards and olive trees which you did
not plant – when you have eaten and are full –
[then] beware, lest you forget יהוה who brought you
out of the land of Egypt, from the house of bondage.

Devarim 8.7-10
For יהוה your God is bringing to a good land; a land
of streams of water, springs, and bursts of water
issuing forth in the valleys and the hills; a land of
wheat and barley, and vines and fig trees and
pomegranates, olive trees for oil, and honey; a land
in which you shall not eat your bread/food in poverty – you shall lack nothing in it; a land whose
stone are iron and from whose hills you will mine
copper; and you shall eat, and you shall be filled,
and you shall bless יהוה your God for the good land
which He has given you.

From these verses, we learn that we are required to
thank יהוה for the food He has provided us.
Hakham Yehudah Hadasi in his *Sefer Eshkol HaKofer,
Davar Anokhi*, Alphabets 1 and 2, wrote concerning the above
verses:

The chief of the prophets said and commanded "And you shall eat, and you shall be filled, and you shall bless יהוה your God..". This utterance does not relate solely that the eater shall bless at the table at specified times when he wants and his body asks. Its law is but for each and every thing that יהוה created in the world... It is obligatory upon you to praise and bless the Creator for each and every thing...

In The *TaNaKh* is says "Shall we accept good from יהוה and not accept bad?" (Iyyov 2.10). From this we can see that just as it is necessary to bless יהוה for the good things that happen to us, so too is it necessary to bless Him for the bad.

Calendar, Festivals, and Holy Days

CHAPTER 8

The Calendar:
Rosh Hodesh and *Aviv*

The determination of the Hebrew calendar – and, hence, the accurate determination of the dates of the Jewish holidays – is dependant on two things the sighting of the new moon, and the sighting of *Aviv* . The sighting of the new moon determines the beginnings and endings of the months of the year, and the sighting of *Aviv* determines the beginning and ending of the year.

Rosh Hodesh: The New Moon

During the time of the Temple, the first day of every lunar month was observed with the blowing of trumpets and a special sacrifice (BeMidbar 10.10; 28.11-15). As a regular, periodic worship day, the new moon is sometimes mentioned in parallel with the Sabbath (Melakhim Bet 4.23); and there is some doubt as to whether *Mela'khah* was prohibited on this day (Amos 8.5).

The sanctification of *Rosh Hodesh* according to sighting the new moon is one of the most important aspects of the festivals. Their accurate timing is dependant on the sighting of the new moon.

> Bere'shit 1.14
> Let there be lights in the firmament of heaven...
> and let them be for Signs and for Holidays.

The importance of the calculation of the new moon is reflected in many aspects of our religious life. In our prayers we declare: "Beginnings of months according to seeing the moon: Truth!" In our marriage contract, the *ketubah*, the bride and groom swear to keep the appointed times of תייהה which are established according to the sighting of the new moon . We have special prayers composed specifically for the day when the new moon has been sighted.

Understanding The New Moon

What is the new moon? How do we know what defines it? Quite simply, the new moon is the first visible crescent of the moon when it has reappeared after its conjunction (a period when the moon apparently disappears in the night sky due to its alignment between the earth and the sun from a given point on earth). Generally, after the moon has reached the point of conjunction, it will renew itself one or two days later in the western horizon shortly after sunset.

For the majority of our history, we have relied strictly on the sighting of the new moon to determine the dates of the holidays. In the Diaspora, this often created differences of opinion between communities, and was a source of some embarrassment when Karaim across the world were celebrating the same holidays on different days! Through the influence of the Bashyachi family, and subsequent Crimean *Hakhamim*, a method of calculating the calendar was developed, and instituted in the Crimea. The purpose of these calculations was to determine the conditions and time when it would be possible to see the new moon, without the interference of random atmospheric factors that prohibit its visibility. The result of these calculations was called the possibility of sighting.

The possibility of sighting was considered equivalent to the actual observation of the new moon except when it was known that it would be impossible to see the new moon given the atmospheric conditions. In those circumstances, it was determined that there was no possibility of sighting; and, despite calculation, the new moon would not be recognized.

While this method was initially intended to account for times when the moon could not be viewed, the method of calculation came to replace actual sighting over time. Eventually, after the Egyptian community had come under the sway of the Crimean community, they, too adopted a system of calculation.

Determining The Months

Today, in the religious leadership in Yisra'el, there is a Court for sanctifying (determining) *Rosh Hodesh* in accordance with Jewish Law. The process of sanctification requires the following:

> Astronomical calculations are carried out by experts in the field in order to determine if the moon will reach a stage on the night in question in which it can be seen or not.

> Eyewitness accounts of sightings of the crescent New Moon as well as sightings of the crescent "Old Moon" (which appears before sunrise shortly before "conjunction") are reviewed in order to determine in what astronomical circumstances a New Moon will be visible to the naked eye.

Phases Of The Moon

In order to describe the position of the Earth in its orbit around the sun, astronomers have chosen an arbitrary starting point in space: The Vernal Equinox (the first day of spring, on which the length of the day and the night are equal). Every day the Earth advances along its orbit away from the point of the Vernal Equinox approximately one degree, until, after a full year, it returns to that same point in space. Astronomers refer to the stage when the moon passes between the Earth and the Sun as conjunction; it is also called the "Astronomical New Moon "(not to be confused with *Rosh Hodesh* , which, in astronomical literature, is often referred to as the "Young Crescent Moon"). During conjunction, the Moon is invisible from the Earth. Over the next fifteen days, the visibility of the Moon from the Earth will continually increase until the Moon is "full". This state is referred to astronomically as opposition. For about two weeks after opposition, the visibility of the Moon wanes until it again reaches conjunction.

Immediately following astronomical conjunction, the Moon continues to remain invisible from the Earth for about a day or two. After this period of time, it becomes visible to the naked eye again in the western horizon. It is this point in time, when the moon is visible again to the naked eye, following conjunction, that we refer to as *Rosh Hodesh* .

The Seven Phases of the Moon

In their literature, our sages divided the phases of the moon described above into seven stages (in Hebrew *Sheva Datot*). The following is a description of each of the seven stages, as described in our *halakhic* (legal) literature:

> Conjunction (also called "its being burnt"), when the moon passes between the Earth and the sun. The moon is not visible from the Earth. Conjunction can be detected from the Earth during a full or partial solar eclipse.

> "From the time of Separation" (also called "its being saved from the burning"), after the moon passes the point of conjunction. The moon remains invisible from the Earth.

> "Appearance of the Moon after sunset" (New Moon), this stage is the time that the moon is first visible after conjunction. This is *Rosh Hodesh* .

"Appearance of the moon with the sun before sunset", in this stage, the moon appears before sunset
and remains visible till moonset.

"The filling of its basin" (Full Moon or Opposition).

"Appearance of the Old", in this stage, the moon
appears in the East before and after sunrise.

"Last Appearance of the Moon ", in this stage, the
moon will appear in the East before sunrise, but
not after; and it will not appear in the East on subsequent days.

In contrast to stage three mentioned above, which is
Rosh Hodesh , the other six stages have no special meaning, and
were therefore ignored.

Calculation

Given that the phases of the moon are well documented,
and the fact that they may be accurately calculated, how do the
calculations of the new moon fit in to the declaration of *Rosh
Hodesh* ? The purpose of calculations to determine the occurrence of the new moon (the possibility of sighting) describe, with
the greatest accuracy, the phases of the moon and sun; however,
they do not necessarily accurately predict when the new moon
can be sighted with the naked eye[32].
There is no *halakhic* (legal) difference between a calculation which is off by one day in determining the time of the

---

32 "Today the Karaites go according to the possibility of sighting which correlates
to actual sightings... they perform the calculation [a calculation to determine
when the new Moon will appear] and, if it turns out that the moon will be visible
in the Horizon after sunset, then they sanctify [the New Moon day]... but, if the
calculation indicates that it will be impossible to see the moon with the naked eye
because of the minuteness of its light then the previous month is reckoned to be
full [30 days long]". – *Hakham* Tuviah Babovitch, Rosh Pinah pg 17.

holidays established by יהוה and a calculation which is off by two days, or ten days: if they are not accurate, the calculations are meaningless.

Sighting

In order to identify any celestial body one must check three pieces of information: The astronomical position of the body, the medium between the body and the observer, and the "Discernment Capability" of the observer.

Astronomical Position

Through astronomical calculations, the position of a celestial body – the time it rises and sets, its distance from the Earth, its distance from the sun, its azimuth (i.e. it angular distance from North), and its height above the horizon, and other relevant factors – may be determined. Calculations often accurately predict a given phase of the moon.

The Medium

A significant factor affecting astronomical observations is what lies between the celestial body and the place of the observation. There are, for example, certain permanent obstructions in the atmousphere, such as the filtering of light passing through the atmousphere, which must be taken into consideration, as well as random obstructions such as clouds, smog, etc,.

Viewing Restrictions

The sighting of the new moon must be done with the naked eye. That was the method used to determine the New Moon in ancient times, and clearly reflects the intent of the Torah, which would not have prescribed an impossible task.

Elements That Affect Moon Visibility

The following criteria are established based on actual observations of the moon from which the different factors affecting visibility are determined. The criteria are only considered reliable if they conform to actual observations, and if not they are meaningless.

Contrast

If the moon is above the horizon, the factor that determines whether it will be visible or not is the ability of the eye to distinguish the moon given the contrast between the light emanating from the moon and the background light of the horizon. In order for the moon to be visible, its light must be greater than the light of the surrounding background. This can be measured in two parameters, namely the "Percentage of Moon's Surface Lit" and the "Moon's Lagtime".

Percentage of the Moon 's Surface Lit

The amount of the moon's surface that is lit and facing us is measured is percentages. As the Percentage Of The Moon 's Surface Lit increases, its brightness increases.

Lagtime

This is the span of time between sunset and moonset. There is a correlation between Lagtime, the height (altitude) of the moon above the horizon at sunset, and the brightness of the background light of the horizon. The greater the Lagtime, the higher the moon will be at sunset, and the weaker the background light will be at moonset.

Taking into account the moon's Lagtime, and the Percentage of Moon 's Surface Lit, we can determine whether or not a "Possibility of Sighting" exists on a given night and how long after sunset the moon will first be visible. The greater the Lagtime, the earlier the moon will first be visible. If the Lagtime is great enough, the moon may first appear before sunset. All the same, there are instances when the moon will be visible before sunset on one day but not visible at all on the previous night. Similarly, the age of the moon can not be determined from the moon's height above the horizon on a given night but only from additional factors such as the season, the speed which the moon moves away from the sun, and the distance of the moon from the Earth and from the sun.

The New Year

The word "*Aviv*" is often misunderstood, due to its use in modern Rabbinic Hebrew to refer to spring. In Biblical Hebrew, the word "*Aviv*" describes barley at a specific point in its development. In legal terms, "*Aviv*" refers to the beginning of the new year (by way of the sighting of barley in the state of *Aviv*).

Aviv And The New Year

The Torah is quite explicit that the sighting of barley in the state of *Aviv* heralds the beginning of the new year:

Shemot 34.18
"The Feast of Unleavened Bread you shall keep. Seven days you shall eat unleavened bread, as I commanded you, in the appointed time of the month of [the] *Aviv*; for in the month of [the] *Aviv* you came out from Egypt..".

Numbers 28.16
'On the fourteenth day of the **first month** [is] the Passover of יהוה...'

Devarim 16.1
"Observe the month of [the] *Aviv*, and keep the Passover to יהוה your God, for in the month of [the] *Aviv* יהוה your God brought you out of Egypt by night..".

The word "*Aviv*" (from the root '-B-B [*Alef-Beit-Beit*], to be fresh) refers to fresh ripening ears of grain (i.e., the state of the grain about 2 or more weeks before it is ready for harvesting). In this specific case, the reference is to the fresh ripening ears of barley in the land of Yisra'el.

Taking a look at exactly what the Torah says about this, in Shemot 9:31-32, in describing the damage done in Egypt by the seventh plague (hail) it is written:

> And the flax and the barley were smitten, because the barley was **Aviv** and the flax was budding. But the wheat and the spelt were not smitten because they late (i.e. they do not head up and ripen until later).

We also have the following:

> Shemot 12:2
> This month/new moon [that after the sighting of *Aviv*] shall be for you the beginning of the months; it shall be for you the first of the months of the yEarthis is followed by the regulations concerning the *Pesah* [Passover] sacrifice to be made at sunset at the end of the fourteenth-beginning of the fifteenth day of the month and *Hagh HaMassot* [the pilgrimage festival of unleavened bread]. In Shemot 13:4 it says:

> This day you are going out (from Egypt), in the month of the **Aviv**

This is followed by the same regulations.

In Shemot 23:15, 34:18, and Devarim 16:1 it again states that the exodus from Egypt occurred in the month of the *Aviv* and that the *Pesah* sacrifice is to be made at sunset at the end of the fourteenth-beginning of the fifteenth day of the month, and

Hagh HaMassot is to be observed for seven days, beginning with the fifteenth of the month.

This, again, is paralleled with the statements in Shemot 12:16, 12:18, Wayyiqra' 23:5, BeMidbar 9:5, 28:16, 33:3, etc. that refer to it as the first month, and that the *Pesah* sacrifice is be made at sunset at the end of the fourteenth-beginning of the fifteenth day of the month, and *Hagh HaMassot* is to be observed for seven days beginning with the fifteenth of the month.

It also says that *Hagh HaMassot* occurs during the barley harvest and that on the Sunday that occurs during the festival the wave offering of the first 'Omer [a measure equal to one tenth of an *Efah*] of barley from the harvest is to be made, and we are to count seven full Sabbaths from then and observe *Hagh HaShavu'ot* [the pilgrimage festival of weeks] on the day after the seventh Sabbath.

The *Aviv* and the following harvesting of barley in Egypt occurs a month earlier than it does in the land of Yisra'el. We learn from Shemot 9:31 that Egypt's barley was *Aviv* and destroyed at the time of the seventh plague. There still remained the coming and going of Mosheh from God to Pharaoh three more times with a plague following each refusal of Pharaoh to let the Yisra'el ites leave. That is then followed by the instructions to take a lamb on the tenth day of the month to be kept until the sunset ending the fourteenth and beginning of the fifteenth of the month at which time it was to be sacrificed, and the following morning the Yisra'el ites were to leave Egypt. Yet these events – which clearly happened after the month in which Egypt's barley, which was *Aviv,* was destroyed – are commanded to occur in the month of the *Aviv* (i.e., the month beginning with the new moon that occurs after the *Aviv* is found in the land of Yisra'el) and the *Pesah* sacrifice (which is commanded to be made in all future generations only in the chosen place, i.e., the Temple in Jerusalem, and forbidden to be made anywhere else) is to be made and *HaghHaMassot* is to be held during that month and that the barley harvest in the land of Yisra'el occurs at the time of the festival. From this it is clear that it is the *Aviv* of the land of

Yisra'el that is the sign that the year begins with the following new moon and not the *Aviv* in any other place in the world.

Being that the calendar of the Torah is a lunar calendar, 12 lunar months is approximately 11 days shorter than a solar year. The ripening of the barley is dependent on the seasons of the solar year and thus occasionally the calendar will contain a thirteenth month (a leap month) so that the first month always occurs after the ripening of the barley in the land of Yisra'el.

Once the *Aviv* has been found in the land of Yisra'el, we can then know exactly when each *Mo'ed* [set time] is to occur relative to it. The year can consist of either 12 or 13 lunar months depending on when the barley is seen to have reached the state of *Aviv*. The state of the barley crops in Yisra'el are usually examined at the end of the 12th month. If the barley is in the state of *Aviv* at this time, then the next month is *Rosh Hodesh Ha-Aviv* – the New Year. If the barley is still immature, it is checked at the end of the 13th month, at which point it has usually reached the state of *Aviv*.

By convention, any year with 13 months is referred to as a leap year. Not to be confused with the leap year of the Gregorian calendar, which adds an extra day to the month of February every four years, the Torah leap year is the addition of an extra month based on the sighting of barley in the state of *Aviv*; and, consequently, the occurrence of a leap year cannot be calculated.

Identifying *Aviv*

Barley which is in the state of *Aviv* has 3 characteristics:

1. It is brittle, and has begun to lighten in color.

2. It is dry enough that it can be eaten parched.

3. It will be harvest-ready 2-3 weeks later.

Not all the barley ripens in the land of Yisra'el at the same time, as might be expected. The new year is determined, then, by the sighting of barley in the state of *Aviv* from the first fields to display signs.

A Note On The Torah Calendar

The true, Biblical calendar does not have month names. Rather, months are referred to by their number (i.e., first month, second month, etc.,), as can be attested to by the following passages:

> Shemot 12.2
> "This month [shall be] your beginning of months; it [shall be] the first month of the year to you.

> Shemot 16.1
> And they journeyed from Elim, and all the congregation of the children of Yisra'el came to the Wilderness of Sin, which is between Elim and Sinai, on the fifteenth day of the second month after they departed from the land of Egypt.

> Wayyiqra' 16.29
> "[This] shall be a statute forever for you: In the seventh month, on the tenth [day] of the month, you shall afflict your souls, and do no work at all, [whether] a native of your own country or a stranger who dwells among you".

> Wayyiqra' 23.34
> "Speak to the children of Yisra'el , saying: 'The fifteenth day of this seventh month [shall be] the Feast of Tabernacles [for] seven days to יהוה.'"

Not once in the Torah is a month given a proper name.

Later on in the *TaNaKh*, names for months are recorded in the book of Kings (Melakhim Aleph 6.1, Melakhim Aleph 6.37-38, Melakhim Aleph 8.2). The names recorded are Bul, Ziv and

Etanim. These names only appear in the book of Melakhim, as listed above; and all of these passages may be found in the account of the construction of the Temple. Many scholars are of the opinion that names are of Phœnician origin. There are many reasons for this. First, the text translates these foreign month names into Torah month names – i.e., "in the month Ziv, which is the second month", etc. Furthermore, Phœnicians (descendants of the Cana'anites) were actively engaged in the building of the Temple (Melakhim Aleph 5).

How do we know these are Phœnician names? This is confirmed by the fact that one of the names Bul, has been found in Phœnician and Cana'anite inscriptions. If we know that Bul is a Phœnician name then most certainly, Ziv and Etanim also are.

CHAPTER 9

The Sabbath

The observance of the Sabbath, *Shabbat* in Hebrew, is central to Jewish life. It gives form and definition to our lives. The observance of *Shabbat* is one of the most significant commandments. The Torah takes Sabbath observance so seriously that violating it entails the death penalty (Exodus 31.14; 35.2; Numbers 15.32). Of the eight holy days in the Torah, only the Sabbath is included in the Decalogue.

Shabbat is our most ancient holiday, originating in the creation itself. According to the Torah, יהוה rested on the seventh day of creation, making it sacred (Genesis 2.1-2). It was that act of rest that was יהוה's final creation, the culmination of the creation process. The Torah teaches us that *Shabbat* serves as a memorial of the order of creation. However, since our liberation from Egypt, it is also a memorial of the Exodus.

Shabbat is usually used to signify the seventh day of the week. However, it may refer to the Sabbath week (Wayyiqra' 23.15-16), or the Sabbatical year (Wayyiqra' 25.1-7) in which the land was to be at complete rest.

Sabbath observance involves the affirmation that יהוה is Creator and Sustainer of the world. If the Creator stopped His creative activity on the seventh day, then those who share in his creative work must do the same. *Shabbat* denies any pride that may accompany our mastery and manipulation of יהוה's creation. In ceasing from labor and entering *Shabbat* one is reminded of the magnificence of יהוה's creation and the insignificance of our own in comparison. We become aware of our true status as

162

dependent beings. We become aware of יהוה who cares for and sustains all his creatures, and of the world as belonging ultimately to יהוה.

The Sabbath is a confirmation of Yisra'el 's identity as יהוה's holy nation. In Devarim 5.12-15 we learn that the Sabbath functions to remind us of our importance to יהוה.

> Devarim 5.15
> "Remember that you were slaves in Egypt and that יהוה your God brought you out of there with a mighty hand and an outstretched arm. Therefore יהוה your God has commanded you to observe the Sabbath day".

Through *Shabbat,* יהוה is recognized as the saving presence in the history of the Jewish people and, through Yisra'el, all of creation. As such, *Shabbat* is a testament of יהוה's faithfulness to His covenant throughout the generations. Our covenant demands holiness; by keeping *Shabbat* we are reminded continually that יהוה who sanctified *Shabbat* also sanctifies us.

Shabbat is a gift. In a modern world, surrounded by busy activities, we often forget how significant a gift this is. Many of us no longer know how to rest. In fact, we have lost the ability to appreciate the sense of community and family that are built, and the sense of spiritual and physical well being that are promoted when *Shabbat* is carefully observed.

The Sabbath is more than just a cessation of labor. It is to be a delight and joy (Yesha'yahu 58.13). We are to celebrate *Shabbat* with festivity, and bring joy to it. Many people reserve their favorite foods for *Shabbat*. Special, joyous songs have been written for *Shabbat*. *Shabbat* is a time to come together with family and friends and share the celebration of יהוה's graciousness.

Karaism and Sabbath Candles: It was Menahem Ben-Yoseif Bashyachi (father of Eliyahu Bashyachi) who first broke with Karaite tradition and permitted Karaim to light candles on *Shabbat*. (It was Menahem, as well, who changed the Torah reading schedule to match that of the Rabbanites). With this innovation, two factions developed in Karaite Constantinople where Bashyachi served as *Dayan* [Judge] – those who would light candles, and those who would not. In general there was, initially, a strong opposition to candle lighting. For example, Avraham Ben Ya'aqov Bali of Adrianople in 1505 wrote a tract entitled, *Igeret Isur Ner Shel Shabbat*, which denounced the admission of this Rabbinic practice. Ultimately, carrying on his father's legacy of promoting Rabbinic practices in Karaism, Eliyahu Bashyachi, through his immense popularity, was able to remove much resistance to candle lighting on *Shabbat* in Turkey, the Crimea and Europe. While this practice was prevalent in Europe, it was rejected in Egypt, as mentioned by Mordehai Ben-Nisan in his Dod Mordehai (fol. 15a). It was not adopted there until the 19th century, after the influence of Crimean practices was more heavily felt there.

Helping to resolve this issue, modern Hakhamim have noted rightly that allowing a lighted candle to burn on *Shabbat* is forbidden. To quote *Hakham HaDayan* Yosef el-Gamil: "The Sages strictly proscribed the lighting of fire from the eve of the Sabbath until the night following the Sabbath in accordance with the verse [from Torah], 'You shall cause no fire to burn throughout your habitations on the Sabbath day...' *Hakham* Eliyahu Bashyachi allowed the lighting of a candle prior to the Sabbath eve; but he was in a minority among the Karaite sages. The communities of Egypt, Syria and Yisra'el were among the strictest [with regard to their observance of the *miswah* (command) of refraining from having fire over *Shabbat*]".33

Mela'khah (Work)

How do we understand work? What is the Torah prohibiting? In Hebrew, the word translated as "work" is "*Mela'khah*". Unfortunately there is no direct equivalent for *Mela'khah* in the English language, and "work", while the closest match is a far

---

33 *Hakham* HaDayan Yosef el-Gamil, "HaYehudot HaQarait BeMisrayim BeAyt

from accurate translation. To learn what *Mela'khah* is we must look to examples.

In the Torah there are only three explicit prohibitions concerning work on the Sabbath.

No fires are to be allowed to burn (Shemot 35.3).

No one is allowed to leave their *moshav* [place: city, town, village, or encampment] (Shemot16.29).

All food was to be prepared [i.e., cooked or baked] in advance of *Shabbat* (Shemot16.23-24).

Aside from explicit injunctions, we also find prohibitions that are implied in the Torah. For example, we are prohibited from performing laborious tasks (BeMidbar 15.32-36).

The Prophets and Writings also shed light on what constitutes *Mela'khah*.

The carrying of a burden is prohibited (Yirmiyahu 17.22).

Buying and selling is prohibited (Nehemyah 13.15-22).

In general, to be safe, we interpret *Mela'khah* in the broadest sense, avoiding whatever might be construed as work, keeping in mind that, while *Mela'khah* is prohibited, this does not mean that all activity is prohibited.

HeHadashah".

On The Sabbath

Preparing For The Sabbath

To be extra careful, one should generally cease all work a little while before sunset (the exact amount of time is indeterminate – mandating a set amount would be adding to Torah, which is forbidden)

All food for the entirety of *Shabbat* must be prepared before *Shabbat* comes in (Shemot 16.23).

As mentioned above, all fires must be extinguished before sunset (Shemot 35.3). However, this implies, among other things, that all incandescent lights have been turned off, and that we don't light candles for *Shabbat*.

While incandescent lights are not permitted, fluorescent lights are, if they are run from a battery operated device. Incandescent lights rely on burning to produce light, which is prohibited as above, while fluorescent lights rely on the excitement of electrons.

There is no electricity used/purchased from the power company, consequently, all electrical devices that must be plugged in to an outlet must be turned off, including heaters, air conditioners and refrigerators (Yesha'yahu 58.13).

Battery operated electrical devices that don't produce a flame or burning are permitted, when turned on before *Shabbat*.

The Sabbath Eve

At sunset *tefillat 'erev* for *Shabbat* is prayed. Following services, people return to their homes, often with guests, for the Sabbath evening meal. The mood around the table, which is well set with food, should be festive, and there are several traditional songs that are sung to accompany the meal.[34]

The Home Ritual and Qiddush

Before the evening meal is begun, someone from the family recites the *qiddush* over grape juice or wine.

After the *qiddush*, the blessing for bread is recited, then the meal begins.

The atmousphere of the Sabbath table should be joyous, and celebratory. It is good to invite guests to your Sabbath meal, and celebrate *Shabbat* with traditional songs, and Torah learning.

After finishing the meal, we say the grace after meals.

The Sabbath Day

During the day, after *tefillat boqer* (at sunrise), we return home to eat our meals. The food served at this meal is eaten cold, and it is comprised of food that was fully prepared before *Shabbat* arrived. Again, it is good to invite guests to the meal, and make the table festive with Torah learning and songs.

---

34 See the Siddur Mequssar Berakhot l'Shabbat [Abbreviated Prayer Book for Sabbath Evening], especially for songs and conducting the home services.

Tasks Forbidden On The Sabbath

It is forbidden to leave the boundaries of one's *moshav* (place: city, town, village, or encampment). This includes crossing natural boundaries (i.e., rivers, streams, etc.), even if the natural boundary runs through one's *moshav* (Shemot 16.29).

Anything that is forbidden to us is also forbidden to anyone performing that act for us – intentionally or not (Shemot 20.10).

It is considered labor on the Sabbath to deliberately and willfully set in motion on Friday some operation that will automatically continue on the Sabbath and will serve the performer of the action on that day. This holds even if the operation is initiated through the giving of an order: if it is generated through a one time action that is then discontinued, or if it is a direct or an indirect act, or if it is complete or incomplete. Examples are the operation of a refrigerator, an electric plate to warm food, or any other, device, electrical or not, that is started on Friday so as to operate on the Sabbath; it may include irrigation, or any other manner of work.

Riding an animal, sailing in a vessel, or traveling in any other vehicle on the Sabbath is forbidden. Someone onboard a sailing vessel over *Shabbat* is not in violation of the Sabbath, but should observe *Shabbat* completely while on board. Boarding a vessel on Friday, prior to *Shabbat* with the intention of being on board the vessel over *Shabbat* is prohibited.

The commandment of circumcision may be performed.

Bathing is not permitted on the Sabbath, even for a *tame'* person; cleansing oneself on the Sabbath is in itself *Mela'khah.*

Every action that is done in excess [so as to cause fatigue] may lead to the desecration of the Sabbath, therefore, such actions are prohibited.

It is forbidden to enjoy the fruits of work done on the Sabbath, whether the work was performed in error or deliberately.

Suspension of Sabbath Rules: Both Karaism and Rabbanism are in complete agreement that danger to life supersedes the Sabbath. This is true in all cases, except when apostasy is at stake.

> Eliyahu Bashyachi, *Aderet Eliyahu, Inyan Shabbat*
> Scholars say that in all matters in which a man's judgment convinces him that his life is in peril, he may violate *Shabbat* on that account, so as to eliminate the danger to his life.

Requirements Of The Sabbath

We are required to remember the Sabbath day, to keep it holy (Shemot 20.8). This entails that we actively make our selves aware of the fact that it is *Shabbat*, during *Shabbat*, so that we refrain from profaning it.

We are required to sanctify the Sabbath day. Our sages have observed that the expression of sanctity or holiness is used in at least two contexts:

Remaining ritually clean (Shemot 20.8, Shemot 19.15, Devarim 5.12). This includes refraining from *Bi'ah* [sexual intercourse].

Mental and spiritual preparation on Friday for the entry of *Shabbat.*

Customs For The Sabbath

It is customary to begin preparing for the Sabbath early Friday morning (Shopping for *Shabbat* is often done on Thursday). First, the food required for *Shabbat* is made, and then the house is cleaned and set in order: the table set, all the power is turned off, the phone is unplugged, etc.,
Some of the customary dishes consumed on *Shabbat* are:

Foul Beans

Matfuna (a dish made from noodles, consumed at festive occasions)

Fried potatoes

Stuffed grape leaves

In the old days, it was customary to store the food for *Shabbat* in a wooden food chest called a *namaliyya.* Today, we either store the food in our refrigerator, using ice packs to keep the food cold (reusable, medical style ice packs are the best), or a food cooler with ice packs (some people will fill their sink with ice, and place their food in an ice chest, with ice in it as well).

Leisure Activities For The Sabbath

We spend the day reading (reading that is not *Mela'khah*), talking (but not about business or

anything thing that could be considered
Mela'khah), going for a stroll (within the confines of
one's *moshav*) and visiting friends, and generally
relaxing.

It is considered noteworthy to study *TaNaKh*, and
other works that help to elevate the spirit on *Shab-bat*.

The things that may be done on the Sabbath are
learned from the scripture, inference and traditional custom. They fall only into the category of
activity. They are: walking, sitting, standing, set-
ting the table for eating, the actual eating and
drinking themselves; the shelling of seeds, nuts
and almonds; the welcoming of visitors and offering food and drink; carrying and studying books;
the washing of feet and hands; dressing; applying
perfume.

At the *beit keneset*, there may be gatherings in the
late afternoon for study and discussion.

Concluding The Sabbath

The Ending of the Day

'*Al pi* Torah [According to the Torah], a day (a 24 hour
day) begins and ends at sunset (c.f. Bere'shit 1: "*Wayyehi 'erev
wayyehi voqer yom ehad,... sheni,...etc*". – "And there was
evening and there was morning, one day,...a second day,...etc".).
Therefore *Shabbat* officially begins and ends at sunset (Heb.
Bein HaArbayim).

Just as we cease work a little bit before *Shabbat*
comes in on Friday we don't recommence
Mela'khah until after *tefillat 'erev* on *Mosa'ei Shab-*

bat, which we begin a while (again no set amount of time) after sunset on Saturday evening.

Havdalah

As *Shabbat* goes out, we perform the *Havdalah* (distinction) service in order to distinguish between the holy and the secular. This service was borrowed from Rabbanism, and has become a custom of the Karaites. It is not a requirement of the Torah, but does serve to provide a ritual boundary for *Shabbat*. The service is conducted as follows: A member of the household, usually the *Ba'al HaBayit* (head of the house), recites the *Havdalah* over a cup of wine, and says a blessing over myrtle. There are also hymns for *Havdalah* that can be sung. [35]

---

[35] See Volume IV (Berakhot) of the Karaite Siddur for the text of the *Havdalah* service, and the hymns for *Havdalah*, or Siddur Mequssar leShabbat.

CHAPTER 10

Passover and The *'Omer*

It is just two weeks into the new year, and the Jewish home is bustling with excitement and frenetic preparation. The house is to be spotless, completely clean and free of any *Hames, Se'or* and *Mahmeset*. The atmousphere is joyous. It is the season of our redemption. Everyone is looking forward to the Passover *seder* with anticipation. Family and friends will gather once again, to celebrate the tale that has been told for thousands of years at this time.

It is four hundred years into the slavery of the sons of Yisra'el living in Egypt. The doorposts of the house are dripping with blood to ward off the death that permeates the night. The atmousphere is tense. It is the night of our redemption. Gathered together in families, the children of Yisra'el eat their Passover meal, a lamb with bitter herbs. The food is consumed hastily, and everyone eats with their sandals on their feet as a sign of their readiness for a quick departure. The death cries of the firstborn of Egypt can be heard all around in the background of the mourning of a nation. These death cries are the birth pangs of a new nation.

The Feast of Unleavened Bread (Hebrew *Hagh HaMassot*), not to be confused with *Pesah* (which was the time of an offering) begins with the evening of Passover, and lasts for one week. For that week, we not only refrain from consuming any leaven: *hames, Se'or* or *Mahmeset*, we remove it from our homes. We hold sacred assemblies on the first and seventh days of the week, and for the whole week, if possible, stay home from our occupations.

> Shemot 12.15
> 'Seven days you shall eat unleavened bread. On the first day you shall remove leaven from your houses. For whoever eats leavened bread from the first day until the seventh day, that person shall be cut off from Yisra'el .

The first and seventh days of *Hagh HaMassot* are festival days. This means that on these days, as on *Shabbat*, no work [*Mela'khah*] may be done – with the noted exception of cooking, which is permitted on festival days. For more information on *Mela'khah*, see the section on *Mela'khah* in Chapter 9.

Historical Notes

The day of Passover is defined by the Paschal sacrifice. During the time of the Temple, there were two different times in the year when the Passover sacrifice could be brought. The first was on the first day of the Festival of Unleavened Bread. If, however, a person was unclean, or on a trip and unable to offer the Passover sacrifice at this time, they were given the opportunity to do so again, at a later date. Importantly, the fact that a given individual was unable to offer the Passover sacrifice did not mean that they did not observe the strictures of *Hagh HaMassot*. They still had to observe every other aspect of Passover and *Hagh HaMassot*, such as removing *hames*, *Se'or* and *Mahmeset*, refraining from consuming them, etc.

The second Passover was celebrated in the second month of the year, on the fourteenth day. The scripture states:

> BeMidbar 9.9-12
> Then יהוה spoke to Mosheh, saying, "Speak to the children of Yisra'el , saying: 'If anyone of you or your posterity is unclean because of a corpse, or

[is] far away on a journey, he may still keep יהוה's Passover. 'On the fourteenth day of the second month, at twilight, they may keep it. They shall eat it with unleavened bread and bitter herbs. 'They shall leave none of it until morning, nor break one of its bones. According to all the ordinances of the Passover they shall keep it.

Differences between the second Passover and the other two Passovers

The eating of unleavened bread for seven days is not obligatory on the second Passover.

The second Passover was not a holy convocation.

The sacrifice of the second Passover was slaughtered in the presence of leaven.

The remaining ordinances of the Passover of the generations and the second Passover are the same.

The Passover of Egypt

The Passover celebration observed by our ancestors in Egypt is different from that we celebrate today in many respects. It is important for us to know and remember the differences between what we celebrate and what they experienced to help us bridge the gap between the two, and hold a better appreciation for the holiday.

A few of the differences between our Passover and the Passover of Egypt are detailed below:

Passover – Egypt	Passover - Generations
Slaughtered in Egypt after the tenth plague, the death of the first-	Slaughtered in the Temple during the period of the Kingdom of Yisra'el.

born.

It was prepared on the tenth of the month.	It was prepared on the fourteenth of the month.
The blood was sprinkled on the lintels and the door posts.	The blood was sprinkled and poured onto the altar.
The text does not relate what was done with the fat of the sacrifice.	The fat was placed on the altar.
It was eaten by both pure and unclean persons.	It was eaten by purified persons only.
It was eaten hurriedly.	It was eaten leisurely.
The Sanctification was not read.	The Sanctification was read.
It was not slaughtered and eaten in a chosen place.	It was slaughtered and eaten in a chosen place.

Prohibited Items: *Hames, Se'or* And *Mahmeset*

In the Torah, there are three different things we are prohibited from consuming, or possessing over *Hagh HaMassot* that are usually lumped together under the catch-all term, "leaven". These items – *Se'or, hames,* and *Mahmeset* – are actually distinct. David b. Abraham al-Fasi's, *Kitab Jami' al-Alfaz* (ed. S.L. Skoss, New Haven, 1936-1945) includes two relevant entries in his dictionary. *HAMES* (vol. 1, p. 560, lines 67-69): mukhtamar ("something leavened"); and *SE'OR* (vol. 2,

p. 300, lines 73-75): *Se'or* = *khamir* ("leaven, sourdough"), *Hames* = *mukhtamar* ("something leavened") and *Mahmeset* = anything that uses (=contains?) *bunn* ("coffee beans"), *kishk* ("*kishk*" – a mixture of bulgar and milk that is dried; for a description check Edward Lane's Manners and Customs of the Modern Day Egyptians), and *kamakh* ("vinegar, pickles"). David al-Fasi's definitions align with one of the views expounded by Yefet Ben-'Eli (Paris Bibliotheque Nationale ms.). See also Aharon Ben Eliyahu, *Sefer Gan 'Eden, Inyan Hagh HaMassot*, ch. 1, fol. 45, col. b[36], and *Adderet Eliyahu, Inyan Hagh HaMassot*, ch 4, Odessa, 1872, fols. 66-67[37].

Hames is anything that has soured, such as vinegar, wine, and leaven. *Hames* is edible.

Shemot 12.15
'Seven days you shall eat unleavened bread. On the first day you shall remove leaven from your houses. For whoever eats *hames* [leavened bread] from the first day until the seventh day, that person shall be cut off from Yisra'el .

Se'or is a mixture that has fermented (literally, it is sour) and therefore can be used for leavening (though not always). For example sour dough starter is *Se'or*. *Se'or* is not edible.

Devarim 16.4
For seven days no *Se'or* shall be found with you in all your territory, and none of the flesh of what you slaughter on the evening of the first day shall be left until morning.

---

36 Aharon distinguishes between *Se'or* (s.th. inedible, which is added to dough to leaven it, i.e. leaven), *Hames* (edible, e.g. bread), and *Mahmeset* (a mixture of *Hames* and something else such as Shekhar HaMadday).

37 Bashyaschi explains that *Hames* refers both to flour mixed with leaven and also to flour mixed with water, which is allowed to rest for a while before being baked. In his definition of *Mahmeset* he explains that *Shekhar HaMadday* is an alcoholic beverage ("like wine") made by immersing leavened bread in water, allowing it to rest (and ferment) in sunlight for many days, and then pounding it.

Mahmeset is a mixture of *hames* or *Se'or* with another item. For example, a seasoning that contains vinegar (which is *Se'or*) would be considered *Mahmeset*.

> Shemot 12.19-20
> 'For seven days no leaven shall be found in your houses, since whoever eats *Mahmeset* [what is leavened], that same person shall be cut off from the congregation of Yisra'el , whether [he is] a stranger or a native of the land.

There are six types of grain that we know can become *hames*:

Wheat	Spelt
Barley	Oats
Rye	Millet

Preparing For Passover

Passover is a holiday that begins, in a sense, before it begins. One of the most important aspects of Passover is its preparation. Many Jewish homes start to buzz with activity about a month before Passover when Passover cleaning begins. Then, after all forbidden foods have been gotten rid of, there is the Passover shopping spree. On top of this, the seder must be planned, invitations sent out, and the old card table and the rickety old folding chairs must be brought up from the basement to make sure that there is room enough for everyone at the seder.

Cleaning

In preparation for Passover, we are obliged to clean our houses thoroughly. This involves the following:

> All *hames*, *Mahmeset* or *Se'or* (leaven) must be consumed, thrown out, or given away, before the

first day of the festival. This includes things such as loaves of bread, pasta, cheese, liquor (including beer *and* wine), vinegar, etc., On the first day of the festival there must be no leaven anywhere in the house/apartment, on the property (this includes animal food), or in other private areas (such as a car, garage, or office space).

The entire house, every corner, must be examined and cleaned for leaven, so that it is not present or seen on the roof of the house, in the courtyard, in the garden, in the store-room, or in any other place.

Any leaven found during cleaning should be deposited outside the house, to be burned, as it is found.

All utensils, plates, and cooking vessels must be thoroughly cleansed, removing handles that are not welded on, and cleaning in crevices where leaven may be lodged.

On the day of Passover eve, before the festival, any remaining leaven is burned.

If the festival falls on a Monday the house cleaning must be completed by Friday, so as not to desecrate the Sabbath.

Making Massah

Traditionally, Karaim have made their own *Massah*. The following steps should be followed when making your own *Massah*:

Sift the flour.

Make sure the flour is not mixed with any chemical compound, in order to avoid fermentation.

Knead the dough in small quantities at a time, as rapidly as possible and immediately put it into a hot oven so that there is no delay between the kneading and the baking.

The dough may not be kneaded with warm or salt water as these cause fermentation.

The dough should be kneaded with pure water only (no fruit juice).

It is forbidden to cook flour, semolina, grits (*"burghul"* in Arabic) or fritters or to make *tagrines* (a traditional Karaite dish); nor may a dough be made from the six leavening grains listed above, in particular millet (whose flour has been proven beyond all doubt to leaven like the others), or from any other grain proved to leaven.

The *Seder*

Shemot 10.2
"and that you may tell in the hearing of your son and your son's son the mighty things I have done in Egypt, and My signs which I have done among them, that you may know that I [am] יהוה".

Shemot 13.8
"And you shall tell your son in that day, saying, '[This is done] because of what יהוה did for me when I came up from Egypt.'

Shemu'el al-Maghribi, *al-Murshid*
It is our duty on this first night, Passover, to recite in our prayer the scriptural passages relating to the Passover. After this, we are to gather in our houses and recite the Biblical verses containing the account of the distressing servitude in which our fathers were living; of the two messengers Mosheh and Aharon ... and of the exodus of the people of Yisra'el from Egypt. We are to make this recitation in the most wondrous manner, and add our own praise to יהוה for all these mercies.

The *seder* is the centerpiece of the first day of Passover. Reading the Passover *Haggadah* is the way Karaites have traditionally fulfilled the commandment to relate the story of the Exodus. The word *seder*, in Hebrew, means order; and in the context of the Passover *seder*, it refers to the rituals and methods we use to tell the story.

The text of the *Haggadah* is taken mostly from Tehillim [Pslams], Bere'shit, Shemot, Yehezq'el, Devarim and Wayyiqra'. It begins with praise to יהוה who redeemed us from our slavery to the Egyptians: "In the Name of the Redeemer who is sought out by all who ask – *Hallelu-Yah*".

The *seder* service, itself, is quite simple. A member of the household, usually the *Ba'al HaBayit* [head of the household] sings the *Haggadah* using the traditional Karaite melody. After he is finished reading the *Haggadah*, the meal is eaten.

Today, in the absence of the Temple, we do not offer the Passover sacrifice. However, in remembrance of the days of the Temple and the Passover sacrifice, many include a lamb roasted on the fire in our Passover *seder*. We eat it with unleavened bread and bitter herbs.

Requirements For Passover

As with all holidays – *Mela'khah a*, except that required to make food, is prohibited (Wayyiqra' 23.7).

Passover is one of the three major pilgrimage festivals, and therefore, during the time of the Temple, all males were required, if able, to go to Yerushalayim for its celebration (Shemot 23.17, Devarim 16.16).

All leaven must be consumed, removed, or destroyed prior to the beginning of the festival of Passover – as above (Shemot 12.19).

On the night of Passover, the Passover *Haggadah* must be read in order to fulfill the commandment that we tell the story of the Exodus to our children (Shemot 10.2).

Customs Of Passover

The following are a few of the customs surrounding Passover and *Hagh HaMassot:*

It is customary to purchase a new tablecloth especially for the Passover *seder.*

Many households have special utensils they use only for *Hagh HaMassot* (pots, pans, cups, flatware, etc.,).

It is customary to eat a lamb, roasted by the *Ba'al HaBayit* [head of the household], for the Passover meal.

The Passover table is set with bitter herbs and *Massah* (a requirement to eat at the Passover meal, not a custom). This *Massah* is made without any special seasonings, such as coriander, that we might feel the poverty of our ancestors in Egypt.

Rice, stuffed grape leaves, and a wide variety of vegetables (leeks, beans, potatoes, corn, etc.,) are also found in the Passover meal.

As wine is forbidden on *Hagh HaMassot* and Passover (wine is *Se'or*), it is customary to make a special "wine" drink from raisins. This drink is made in the following way: A quantity of raisins are soaked in water (distilled water will work best) less than twenty-four (24) hours before the reading of the *Haggadah* (to avoid fermentation [*Se'or*]). The raisins are crushed, and a brown juice is extracted through a sieve. This drink is made daily throughout *Hagh HaMassot*.

Requirements For *Hagh Hamassot*

The following requirements apply to the observance of the intermediate days [*Hol HaMo'ed*] of *Hagh HaMassot*, the days between Passover and *Shevi'i Aseret*:

It is commendable if one does not work at their occupation during the intermediate days of *Hagh HaMassot*, but this is not required.

We are required to eat some *Massah* on each day of *Hagh HaMassot*: "Seven days you shall eat *Massah...*" (Shemot 12.15).

The 'Omer

Wayyiqra' 23.9-16
'When you come into the land which I give to you, and reap its harvest, then you shall bring a sheaf of the *bikkurim* of your harvest to the priest. 'He shall wave the sheaf before יהוה, to be accepted on your behalf; on the day after the Sabbath the

priest shall wave it... 'You shall eat neither bread nor parched grain nor fresh grain until the same day that you have brought an offering to your God; [it shall be] a statute forever throughout your generations in all your dwellings. 'And you shall count for yourselves from the day after the Sabbath, from the day that you brought the sheaf of the wave offering: seven Sabbaths shall be completed. 'Count fifty days to the day after the seventh Sabbath; then you shall offer a new grain offering to יהוה.

Fro m the first Sunday that occurs during the holiday of Passover, we begin to count the days – literally. This time is often referred to as *Hanafat Ha'Omer*, The Counting of the *'Omer* – or, simply, The *'Omer*. The term "The Counting of the *'Omer*" has arisen from the fact that we are no longer able to bring offerings to the Temple; and, therefore, counting the days between Passover and *Shavu'ot* is the only aspect of the *miswah* we are able to fulfill. However, it is important for us to remember that this was the time of the offering of the firstfruits – the first of the harvest, in Hebrew the *bikkurim* or *reshit qasir* ("beginning of harvest").

Two to three weeks after the beginning of the first month of the year, the barley in the land of Yisra'el was beyond the stage of *Aviv* and was ready to be brought as the wave offering.

Wayyiqra' 23.10-11
"When you come to the land which I give you, and harvest its harvest, you will bring the sheaf of the beginning of your harvest to the priest. And he will wave the sheaf before יהוה so you will be accepted; on the morrow after the Sabbath the priest will wave it".

The offering of *bikkurim* occurred not only in conjunction with Passover at the time of the barley harvest, but there was also an offering of *bikkurim* associated with *Shavu'ot*

(BeMidbar 28.26-31) in celebration of the wheat harvest. The *bikkurim* were brought before יהוה at various times in the course of the agricultural year, but there was a special *bikkurim* festival every year in conjunction with Passover, seven weeks before *Shavu'ot* (Wayyiqra' 23.15).

The Torah does not specifically link the offering of *bikkurim* with the Exodus; however, Devarim 26.1-11 states that when the *bikkurim* is brought before the priest, one is to acknowledge that יהוה had delivered them from Egypt and had given them the land just as He had promised.

Importantly, Yirmiyahu 2.3 states that Yisra'el was "holy to יהוה, the *bikkurim* (*resit*) of his harvest". The image implies that Yisra'el is unique among the nations as the special possession of יהוה; and it is good for us to remember this during The *'Omer*.

During the fifty days of the counting of The *'Omer*, we have a custom to beg for יהוה's mercy that He bring forth the fruit of the Earth for us in peace and blessing. On the fiftieth day, new produce is received and we thank יהוה that the Earth has yielded the crop with blessing and peace. From that new crop an offering was given to יהוה.

How we Count

The counting of The *'Omer* takes place in the morning (Wayyiqra' 23.15). Each person in the family, who is able to count should participate. Usually, the *'Omer* is counted during the morning tefilah. For those unable to attend a morning service, for any reason, the counting may be found in Volume I (*Hol*) of our *Siddur*, pages 88, 89, and 90.

Requirements For The *'Omer*

Each person who is able to sufficiently talk for themselves is required to count the *'Omer* each day.

If a person forgets to count the 'Omer for a particular day, they should resume counting from the day they remember.

Shevi'i 'Aseret

The last day of Hagh HaMassot is a holiday. All the strictures of a holiday apply to Shevi'i 'Aseret. After Shevi'i 'Aseret, hames, Mahmeset and Se'or may be eaten again.

CHAPTER 11

Shavu'ot

The Feast of Weeks, in Hebrew *Shavu'ot*, occurs seven full weeks after the elevation offering of the *bikkurim*. It celebrates the end of the grain harvest. *Shavu'ot* is the only holiday that is not set on a specific day, but always occurs on a specific day. Sound confusing? It isn't. Very simply, the Torah does not dictate on what day of the month *Shavu'ot* must be held (as with Passover, which must be on the fourteenth day of the first month); however, it does dictate, by implication, that *Shavu'ot* will always occur on Sunday – a specific day of the week.

The celebration of *Shavu'ot* is focused around the elevation offerings that were brought to the Temple. Devarim 16.10 stipulates that individuals were to make an offering in proportion to the size of the harvest they had taken in that year; however, Wayyiqra' 23.17-20 and BeMidbar 28.27-30 give much more detailed lists of what the priests were to offer on behalf of the nation. Following the stipulations in Wayyiqra' (the two lists differ slightly), this included burnt offerings of seven male lambs, one bull, and two rams, followed by a purification offering of one goat and a fellowship offering of two lambs. It is a festival day of sacred assembly in which no *Mela'khah*, with the exception of *Mela'khah* required to make food, is permitted.

As not all the barley ripens in the Land of Yisra'el at the same time, the elevation offering is a national sacrifice brought from the first fields to become harvest-ready. The *bikkurim* was brought by individual farmers, and it can vary in ripeness anywhere from in the state of *Aviv* to fully ripe grain which may be brought "crushed" or "coarsely ground":

> Wayyiqra' 2.14
> "And when you bring a first-fruit offering to יהוה; you shall bring your first-fruit offering as *Aviv* parched in fire or crushed Carmel" (Carmel is grain which has hardened to the point where it can only be crushed or coarsely ground).

The Feast of Weeks commemorates two closely related events: The conquest of the land of Yisra'el , and the sowing of the land of Yisra'el with seeds. For the land to yield its crops, יהוה's blessing is necessary, and יהוה's blessing depends upon the fulfillment of the commandments.

Requirements For *Shavu'ot*

> As with all holidays – *Mela'khah*, except that required to make food, is prohibited (Wayyiqra' 23.21).

> *Shavu'ot* is one of the three major pilgrimage festivals, and therefore, during the period of the Temple, all males are required, if able, to go to Yerushalayim for its celebration (Devarim 16.16).

> Services are held at the synagogue (additional prayers for the holiday are included).

Customs of *Shavu'ot*

> A special menu is customarily prepared for *Shavu'ot*, containing dairy products and honey, that symbolizes our hopes for the New Year. Food from the new crops are also included, as well as some dried fruits left over from Passover.

A customary treat, called *'aliluz*, is prepared from *tahor* sugar, lemon and almonds. From this mixture, a syrupy paste is made.

CHAPTER 12

Yom Teru'ah

Wayyiqra' 23.23-24
יהוה spoke to Mosheh, saying: Speak to the Yisra'el
ite people thus: In the seventh month, on the first
day of the month, you shall observe complete rest,
a sacred occasion commemorated with shouting
[teru'ah].

BeMidbar 29.1
In the seventh month, on the first day of the
month, you shall observe a sacred occasion: you
shall not work at your occupations. You shall observe it as a day of shouting.

The first day of the seventh month is a holiday with a sacred assembly and special sacrifice (Wayyiqra' 23.23-25; BeMidbar 29.1-6). BeMidbar 29.1 states that this day is "a day of
shouting" (yom teru'ah). The word teru'ah can also mean a "war-
cry" Yehoshu'ah 6.5, a "shout of joy" (Shemu'el Aleph 4.5), or a
trumpet blast (BeMidbar 10.1-10).

All kinds of noise created by musical instruments such as
the trumpet or shofar are not used today, in respect for the fact
that we have no Temple and we do not offer sacrifices.

Requirements For *Yom Teru'ah*

As with all holidays – *Mela'khah*, except that required to make food, is prohibited.

Services are held at the synagogue for the holiday, which are attended by the community.

Customs Of *Yom Teru'ah*

There are very few customs associated with *Yom Teru'ah;* however, a few are:

For the meal on *Yom Teru'ah* a vegetable as green as myrtle leaves is included, over which a blessing is made (apart from the regular blessing over foods).

Special additions are made to the prayer services on *Yom Teru'ah.*

CHAPTER 13

Yom HaKippurim and the Ten Days

The Ten Days Of Repentance

Ten days separate *Yom Teru'ah*, and *Yom HaKippurim* . During that period of time, it is customary for Karaites to hold special prayer services early in the morning (while it is still night), called *"Selihot"*. The *Selihot* services contain propitiatory prayers, confession and supplication, and in them we beg יהוה to forgive us for our sins. These exercises are intended to prepare our minds and our souls for the holiday to come (*Yom HaKippurim*).

Yom Hakippurim

Yom HaKippurim [The Day of Atonement] is our most solemn holy day. On it we lament in atonement for the sin of our people. It is described in detail in Wayyiqra' 16, and more briefly in Wayyiqra' 23.26-32 and BeMidbar 29.7-11. The Hebrew name *"Yom HaKipurim"* has been popularized as *"Yom Kippur"*.

Yom HaKippurim occurs on the tenth day of the seventh month, and is rich with symbolism. Briefly, the details of the ceremony as conducted by the high priest (*kohen gadol*) in the Temple are as follows. The *kohen gadol* would first bathe and then put on white undergarments and a white tunic; he would not wear his ceremonial insignia. He offered a bull for the sin of himself and his house, and then took a censer with burning coals and incense into the Holy of Holies and sprinkled some blood

194

from the bull on the ark of the covenant. He cast lots over two goats; one would be sacrificed for the sin of the people and the other became the goat for *azazel*. He sacrificed the goat for the sin of the people and sprinkled some of its blood on the ark. He then came out of the tent and cleansed the altar with the blood of the bull and the goat. Then, he put his hands on the head of the goat for *azael* and confessed the sins of the people over it. At that point, an appointed man took the goat for *azazel* out into the wilderness and released it. He had to wash his clothes and bathe before he could return to the camp. The *kohen gadol* would leave his white clothing in the tent of meeting, bathe again, and then put on his regular priestly apparel. The bull and goat that had been sacrificed were to be burned entirely.

Aspects of the symbolism of the ceremony are fairly transparent in meaning. By bathing before entering the tent of meeting, the *kohen gadol* avoided bringing any form of contamination into it. In wearing linen garments rather than his regular priestly insignia, he showed himself penitent, one who had stripped himself of all dignity. The clearest statement of the *kohen gadol's* personal sinfulness was his sacrifice of a bull for the sin of himself and his family.

The real heart of the ceremony, however, and the real point of controversy, is the two goats: one goat for sacrifice, and one goat for *azazel*. Two issues are at stake here. First, what is the meaning of the "goat for *azazel*?" Second, what does this ceremony say about the Torah's concept of atonement?

Several interpretations of the goat for *azazel* have been proposed. A common interpretation, with little foundation in *miqra'* [scripture], is that *azazel* is a goat-demon of the desert. Another interpretation is that *azazel* refers to a cliff from which the goat would be thrown; this, too, is a forced interpretation. Others, take *azazel* to mean "destruction", and thus understand the goat for *azazel* to be a goat that will be destroyed. However, if the goat was simply to be killed in the wilderness one might have expected the text to use more conventional language.

A traditional interpretation, however, that is still worthy of acceptance is that *azazel* is the "scapegoat", that is, a goat to be sent away. This interpretation is found in the Vulgate (*capro emissario*) and the Septuagint (*apopompaio),* and is based on taking *azazel* as a combination of ʻ*ez* ("goat") and *azal* ("depart"). As such, *azazel* is a technical term for a goat taken out and released in ritual fashion. Verse eight speaks of one goat for (i.e., as a sacrifice to) יהוה and one goat for (i.e., to serve as) the scapegoat. This interpretation is in accord with normal Hebrew grammar. To understand this better, one must understand the concept of propitiation in the Torah.

The foundational command for the entire ritual of the Day of Atonement, moreover, is that the *kohen gadol* must not come into the Most Holy Place whenever he chooses or else he will die (Wayyiqra' 16.2). The ceremony allows the *kohen gadol* to propitiate יהוה in order that he may enter יהוה's presence and not be destroyed.

If one acknowledges the reality of propitiation in Torah theology, one may see more clearly the two great aspects of atonement that are portrayed in the ritual of the Day of Atonement. The first is propitiation, as illustrated by the sacrifice of the one goat chosen by lot to be a purification offering. The slaughter of this goat and the sprinkling of its blood on the mercy seat of the ark ritually appeased יהוה's anger. The second is expiation, the removal of sin so that it was forgotten and no longer clung to the people. This was ritually carried out by the scapegoat, who was released far out in the desert to carry sin away. It is significant that the scapegoat was not sacrificed. The scapegoat did not pay the penalty for sin or appease the wrath of יהוה; it carried sin away and was a living parable of the promise that, "As far as east is from west, so far has he removed our transgressions from us" (Tehillim 103.12). The two goats symbolized both propitiation and expiation and together illustrate what atonement means.

Fasting

A question often arises, how do we know that the Torah is asking us to fast on *Yom HaKippurim* ? When speaking of this issue the Torah states: "You shall afflict your souls". The word souls here, is often mistranslated. A cursory look at several other passages in scripture will reveal the fact that the word soul (*nefesh*) is used to talk of a person: a soul and body, as the text states:

> Bere'shit 14.21
> And the king of Sodom said unto Abram, Give me the persons, and take the goods for yourself. {persons: Heb. souls}

> Shemot 12.16
> And in the first day [there shall be] a holy convocation, and in the seventh day there shall be a holy convocation to you; no manner of work shall be done in them, save [that] which every man must eat, that only may be done of you. {man: Heb. soul}

Given this understanding of the text, we should now read it "You shall afflict your person", understanding that this refers both to our body and our soul. How then do we afflict our bodies without violating the Torah? We fast. Furthermore, our Sages noted that the *TaNaKh* considers mortification of the soul fasting:

> Aharon Ben-Eliyahu, Gan 'Eden, *Yom HaKippurim*
> The mortification required on that day [*Yom HaKippurim*] consists of abstention from food and drink, since all affliction of the soul mentioned in connection with the soul signifies fasting, as it is written: "I have afflicted my soul with fasting", (Tehillim 35.13), and, "satisfy the afflicted soul", (Yesha'yahu 58.10)

The fast is from evening to evening, in accordance with the Torah calculation for a day. The terms of the fast day apply to all -- men and women, old or young although, regarding sick people, the fasting depends on their ability to sustain it. Just as saving life supersedes the Sabbath, so does saving life supersede the Day of Atonement. As for children, it is good to get them accustomed to fast as much as they are able, for the Torah commandment is that all Yisra'el afflict themselves in this way.

Our sages formulated twelve guidelines a person should follow in order to attain full expiation. These are:

To express regret[38] for his wicked act.

To express hatred and abhorrence for it; to keep his distance from it in the future.

To repent immediately the moment remorse for the misdeed is felt. He should not say: "I shall sin, and repent for it later", meaning on the Day of Atonement.

To confess to sins.

To submit to his Maker by afflicting the soul (body), that is, by fasting.

To reject wickedness.

To undertake not to commit the deed again.

At the time of the Temple, repentance was accompanied by sacrifice; in the Diaspora it is by prayer: "And we shall offer the calves of our lips".

To leave the evil-doer to his evil.

Not to imitate the evil-doer.

---

38 To be remorseful and ask, "Why did I do this?"

To repent in order to avoid punishment for the deed. Repentance erases the penalty that has to be paid.

Return to total repentance, as this is a positive command of the Torah.

Of course, everyone should be aware of their actions at all times, and if they have violated the Torah, they should repent. Repentance is open to everyone, at all times, and it erases all sins. However, the atonement of this day is special. It is not just atonement for the individual, but atonement for the community as well. Therefore, even one who had not sinned at all would still be required to mourn and ask for forgiveness on *Yom HaKippurim* , as if they had sinned, because every Jew is part of the nation of Yisra'el .

Requirements For *Yom Hakippurim*

Unlike other non-*Shabbat* holidays, **all** *Mela'khah* is forbidden on *Yom HaKippurim* (Wayyiqra' 23.31).

Eating, drinking, and the smelling of spices is refrained from for twenty-six (26) or twenty-seven hours (27) – until about an hour after the sunset of the next day and the evening prayer (Wayyiqra' 23.32).

The attitude of *Yom HaKippurim* is one of remorse, and repentance. (Wayyiqra' 23.29).

Customs Of *Yom Hakippurim*

It is customary to arrive early to the synagogue on the eve of *Yom HaKippurim* .

One should refrain from wearing adornments such as jewelry, makeup, and perfume or cologne.

The meal eaten before *Yom HaKippurim* ("the last meal"), is traditionally comprised of *hamad, guz watum*, potatoes with beetroot, sweet potato, *fariq*, rice pudding, *queshq*, and rice with beetroot.

CHAPTER 14

Sukkot

The Feast of Booths /Tabernacles, in Hebrew *Sukkot*, takes place five days after *Yom HaKippurim* . The festival is described in Wayyiqra' 23.33-43 and Devarim 16.13-15, but the most elaborate presentation is found in BeMidbar 29.12-40.

For seven days we are required to live in *sukkot* (booths). The purpose for living in the booths is to recall the sojourn of our ancestors in the desert prior to their taking of the land of Cana'an.

> Wayyiqra' 23.39-43
>
> ... on the fifteenth day of the seventh month, when you have gathered in the fruit of the land, you shall keep the feast of יהוה [for] seven days; on the first day [there shall be] a sabbath-[rest,] and on the eighth day a sabbath-[rest.] And you shall take for yourselves on the first day the fruit of *hadar* trees, branches of palm trees, the boughs of leafy trees, and willows of the brook; and you shall rejoice before יהוה your God for seven days. You shall keep it as a feast to יהוה for seven days in the year. [It shall be] a statute forever in your generations. You shall dwell in booths for seven days. All who are native Yisra'el ites shall dwell in booths, that your generations may know that I made the children of Yisra'el dwell in booths when I brought them out of the land of Egypt: I [am] יהוה your God.

So Mosheh declared to the children of Yisra'el the feasts of יהוה.

Sukkot is a time of joy. It is a final celebration of and thanksgiving for the year's harvest.

Devarim 16.13-15
You shall observe the Feast of Tabernacles seven days, when you have gathered from your threshing floor and from your winepress. And you shall rejoice in your feast, you and your son and your daughter, your male servant and your female servant and the Levite, the stranger and the fatherless and the widow, who [are] within your gates. Seven days you shall keep a sacred feast to יהוה your God in the place which יהוה chooses, because יהוה your God will bless you in all your produce and in all the work of your hands, so that you surely rejoice.

During the time of the Temple, *'olim* [burnt offerings] were brought on all the seven days of *Sukkot*. The *'olah* [offering] of the first day was thirteen bulls, two rams, and fourteen male lambs, with one goat as a *hatta'ah* [purification offering]. Each day thereafter the number of bulls offered was decreased by one. The eighth day was exceptional: one bull, one ram, seven lambs, and one goat were offered (BeMidbar 29.12-38). These were all in addition to the grain offerings and freewill offerings (BeMidbar 29.39). The series of offerings for this week constituted an extraordinary expense (71 bulls, 15 rams, 105 lambs, and 8 goats). An *'olah* was entirely consumed by fire; even the priests could not eat it.

The prophet Zekharyah looks forward to a time when all the nations will join Yisra'el in participating in *Hagh HaSukkot* and the worship of יהוה.

Zekharyah 14.16-19
And it shall come to pass [that] everyone who is left of all the nations which came against Yerushalayim shall go up from year to year to worship the King, יהוה of hosts, and to keep the Feast of Tabernacles. And it shall be [that] whichever of the families of the Earth do not come up to Yerushalayim to worship the King, יהוה of hosts, on them there will be no rain. If the family of Egypt will not come up and enter in, they [shall have] no [rain;] they shall receive the plague with which יהוה strikes the nations who do not come up to keep the Feast of Tabernacles. This shall be the punishment of Egypt and the punishment of all the nations that do not come up to keep the Feast of Tabernacles.

Requirements For *Sukkot*

Sukkot is one of the three major pilgrimage festivals, and therefore, during the period of the Temple, all males are required, if able, to go to Yerushalayim for its celebration (Devarim 16.16).

We are commanded on this festival to take produce from *hadar* trees, fronds of date palms, and willow branches in order to rejoice before יהוה our God (that is, in the Temple – Wayyiqra' 23.39-41). The *TaNaKh* teaches us that these are to be used in the construction of the *Sukkah* (Nehemyah 8.15).

We are obliged to make *sukkot* – wherever we are able: in our courtyards, on the roofs of their houses, or in any other place. Two or more neighbors may construct the booth jointly (Wayyiqra' 23.42).

We are required to live in the *sukkah* as well as to eat, drink, read, and pray there. None of the seven days of the festival may pass without living in the *sukkah* (Wayyiqra' 23.42).

The *sukkah* must also be under the open sky, spacious enough to accommodate all who wish to enter it.

The *sukkah* must have a roof that is covered entirely with branches.

The *sukkah* should be decorated with the choicest fresh fruit.

Customs Of *Sukkot*

The *sukkah* is traditionally decorated with colorful cloths. Its roofing is made out of freshly cut branches, strewn across the top in a haphazard meshwork.

The booth should be built in the open, and it should have the shape of a house, with a door and door post... Its size should be sufficient for a person to sit and lie comfortably, but one may make it as large as one is able to. (Aharon Ben-Eliyahu, *Sefer Gan Eden, Sukkot*)

Inside the *sukkah*, are palm fronds, willow branches, myrtle, olive leaves, citrus fruits and pomegranates.

To the east of the *sukkah*, a special hanging is placed that reads: "You shall dwell in booths for seven days. All who are native Yisra'el ites shall dwell in booths". (Wayyiqra' 23.42).

Each night, an oil lamp is lit inside the *sukkah* to symbolize the light of the festival.

Shemini 'Aseret

The Eighth Day of Assembly – in Hebrew *Shemini 'Aseret*, also known as *Simhat Torah* (Rejoicing of the Law) – falls on the day following the seven days of *Sukkot,* the 22nd day of the seventh month:

Wayyiqra' 23.36
...On the eighth day [after *Sukkot*] you shall observe a sacred occasion and bring an offering by fire to יהוה; it is a solemn gathering: you shall not work at your occupations.

Shemini 'Aseret is a time of gathering for the Jewish people, as scripture notes:

Melakhim Alef 8.66
On the eighth day he let the people go. They bade the king good-bye and went to their homes, joyful and glad of heart over all the goodness that יהוה had shown to His servant David and His people Yisra'el .

Divrei HaYamim B. 7.10
On the twenty-third day of the seventh month he dismissed the people to their homes, rejoicing and in good spirits over the goodness that יהוה had shown to David and Solomon and His people Yisra'el .

Requirements For *Shemini 'Aseret*

Like other non-*Shabbat* holidays – all *Mela'khah*, except what is required to prepare food – is forbidden.

Customs Of *Shemini 'Aseret*

On this day we complete the reading of the Torah, and recommence our cycle with a reading from the story of creation from the book of Bere'shit.

All the young students that have completed a level of their Hebrew studies, walk in a procession to the synagogue. Each child, girl and boy, are covered with a *Tallit*. The girls are dressed in white, and hold candles and flowers. As they walk, they sing special songs for the occasion, taken from Torah. When the children reach the synagogue, they enter the sanctuary, with the adults who are waiting for them with silver lamps and finials.

After the procession of the children has finished, the Torah scrolls are taken out of the *Aron* [Ark], and are carried around the synagogue in a procession. As the procession proceeds, hymns for *Shemini 'Aseret* are recited. Also, during the procession, each of the mentioned boys and girls read a portion of a verse from Torah, which is completed by the congregation in antiphonal response.

CHAPTER 15

Later Biblical Holidays, Minor Fast Days and National Holidays

Purim

Ester 9.26-28
So they called these days *Purim*, after the name *Pur*. Therefore, because of all the words of this letter, what they had seen concerning this matter, and what had happened to them, the Jews established and imposed it upon themselves and their descendants and all who would join them, that without fail they should celebrate these two days every year, according to the written [instructions] and according to the [prescribed] time, [that] these days [should be] remembered and kept throughout every generation, every family, every province, and every city, that these days of *Purim* should not fail [to be observed] among the Jews, and [that] the memory of them should not perish among their descendants.

Purim was established to celebrate the failure of a courtier of king Ahashverosh of Persia named Haman from destroying the Jewish people. *Purim* is a very joyous time in the Jewish year. Jews from all over the world gather at the synagogue to eat, dance, and be merry. Traditionally, the story of

Ester is read on *Purim*, and children will dress up in costumes, and perform a play based on the story of Ester. As one might expect, one of the favorite costumes for girls on *Purim* is Queen Ester.

The word *"Purim"* means "lots" and refers to the lots Haman cast in order to find a favorable day for the destruction of the Jewish race (Ester 9.18-28).

We observe *Purim* for two days, as it is written: "...the Jews established and imposed it upon themselves and their descendants and all who would join them, that without fail they should celebrate these two days every year, according to the written [instructions] and according to the [prescribed] time". (Ester 9.27). The festival takes place on the fourteenth and fifteenth days of the twelfth month.

Requirements For *Purim*

The days of *Purim* are days of feasting and gladness (Ester 9.18). We should celebrate them, therefore, with feasting, song and dance.

On both days of *Purim*, we are required to have a festive meal (Ester 9.27-32).

On *Purim* we send presents of food to one another, called *mishlo'ah manot* (Ester 9.19).

We are also required to give gifts to the poor.

Customs Of *Purim*

Preparations and even the celebration of *Purim* can begin before the arrival of the festival itself. Sweets are made, costumes are selected and sewn, and the *se'udot* [meals] for *Purim* are planned.

Some traditional desserts served on *Purim* are *wedan Haman* (Haman's ears), *bughashah* (a cream filled strudel), and *zalabiyya* (a doughnut like pastry coated with sugar and rose water).

Candles, traditionally made from bees wax, are ceremonially lit and placed on a special table with holes to hold them; this is because *Purim* is considered a festival of lights (Ester 8.16).

Engagements are often announced on *Purim*.

People try to take *Purim* off from work, or, if they are shop owners, close their shops on *Purim*.

The *Ba'al HaBayit* [head of the household] gives a gift to each family member.

Fast Days

In the history of our people many sorrows have befallen us. The greatest misfortune we have had to bear is the destruction of Yerushalayim, the burning of the Temple, and the exile of our people from their land. Remorsefully, we must admit that it was through our own faults as a nation that we were exiled. Our ancestors were repeatedly warned of the danger they faced if they did not live up to the covenant they entered into with יהוה; but they did not listen.

> Wayyiqra' 26.31-33
> I will lay your cities waste and bring your sanctuaries to desolation, and I will not smell the fragrance of your sweet aromas... I will scatter you among the nations and draw out a sword after you; your land shall be desolate and your cities waste.

In memorial of the destruction of the Temple (known in Hebrew as the *Hurban*) the Jewish nation undertook to observe the anniversary of these disasters as fast days.

Dates And Events Related To The *Hurban*

The fast of the tenth month: the siege of Yerushalayim

> The relevant text is:

> Yirmiyahu 52.3-4
> For because of the anger of יהוה [this] happened in Yerushalayim and Judah, till He finally cast them out from His presence. Then Zedekiah rebelled against the king of Babylon. Now it came to pass in the ninth year of his reign, in the tenth month, on the tenth [day] of the month, [that] Nebuchadnezzar king of Babylon and all his army came against Yerushalayim and encamped against it; and [they] built a siege wall against it all around.

The fast of the fourth month: the breach of the walls of Yerushalayim

> The relevant text is:

> Yirmiyahu 52.6-11
> By the ninth day of the fourth month, the famine had become acute in the city; there was no food left for the common people.
> Then [the wall of] the city was breached. All the soldiers fled; they left the city by night through the gate between the double walls, which is near the king's garden—the Chaldæns were all around the city—and they set out for the Arabah. But the Chaldæan troops pursued the king, and they

overtook Zedekiah in the steppes of Jericho, as his entire force left him and scattered. They captured the king and brought him before the king of Babylon at Riblah, in the region of Hamath; and he put him on trial. The king of Babylon had Zedekiah's sons slaughtered before his eyes; he also had all the officials of Judah slaughtered at Riblah. Then the eyes of Zedekiah were put out, and he was chained in bronze fetters. The king of Babylon brought him to Babylon and put him in prison, [where he remained] to the day of his death.

The fasts of the fifth month: the destruction of the Temple.

The relevant text is:

Mela'khim Beit 25.8-9
On the seventh day of the fifth month—that was the nineteenth year of King Nebuchadnezzar of Babylon—Nebuzaradan, the chief of the guards, an officer of the king of Babylon, came to Yerushalayim. He burned the House of יהוה, the king's palace, and all the houses of Yerushalayim; he burned down the house of every notable person.

There is another fast in the fifth month for the same event:

Yirmiyahu 52.12-13
On the tenth day of the fifth month—that was the nineteenth year of King Nebuchadrezzar, the king of Babylon—Nebuzaradan, the chief of the guards, came to represent the king of Babylon in Yerushalayim. He burned the House of יהוה, the king's palace, and all the houses of Yerushalayim;

he burned down the house of every notable person.[39]

The fast of the seventh month: confession for transgressions.

The relevant text is:

Nehemyah 9.1-3
On the twenty-fourth day of this month, the Yisra'el ites assembled, fasting, in sackcloth, and with Earth upon them. Those of the stock of Yisra'el separated themselves from all foreigners, and stood and confessed their sins and the iniquities of their fathers. Standing in their places, they read from the scroll of the Teaching of יהוה their God for one-fourth of the day, and for another fourth they confessed and prostrated themselves before יהוה their God.

Some hold that this fast is to commemorate the murder of Gedalyahu Ben Elisha, a descendent of the Davidic dynasty. This view is based on the following text:

Melakhim Beit [2 Kings] 25.25
In the seventh month, Ishmael son of Nethaniah son of Elishama, who was of royal descent, came with ten men, and they struck down Gedaliah and he died; [they also killed] the Judeans and the Chaldæans who were present with him at Mizpah.

---

39 It is assumed that on the seventh of this month, the burning of the Temple began, and by the tenth of the month, it was completely destroyed.

Observing The Fasts Today

After seventy years of exile, many Jews returned to Si-yyon [Zion] from Babylon to rebuild the house of יהוה in Yerushalayim. This was at the order of Cyrus, king of Persia (Ezra 1.1-3), who restored many of the conquered peoples under his rule to their lands.

When the building of the second Temple was complete the people put the following question to the priests and the prophets: "Should the fast commemorating the destruction of the Temple, observed by the people for the previous seventy years, continue to be upheld?" (Zekharyah 7.3). The answer from יהוה was as follows:

Zekharyah 7.4-6
Thereupon the word of יהוה of Hosts came to me: Say to all the people of the land and to the priests: When you fasted and lamented in the fifth and seventh months all these seventy years, did you fast for my benefit? And when you eat and drink, who but you does the eating, and who but you does the drinking?

The book of Zekharyah also states:

Zekharyah 8.19
Thus said יהוה of Hosts: The fast of the fourth month, the fast of the fifth month, the fast of the seventh month, and the fast of the tenth month shall become occasions for joy and gladness, happy festivals for the House of Judah; but you must love honesty and integrity.

Other than those fasts mentioned above (and that of *Yom HaKippurim*) we celebrate no other fasts. The require-ments for a minor fast day, with the exception of the fact that

Mela'khah is permitted, are the same as those of *Yom HaKippurim.*

Secular National Holidays

The establishment of the State of Yisra'el in 1948, and the subsequent redemption of the city of Yerushalayim by the modern State of Yisra'el in 1967 saw the creation of new national holidays.

Yom Ha'Asma'ut and Yom HaZikaron

Yom Ha'Asma'ut is a national holiday celebrated in Yisra'el much the same way that other countries celebrate their independence day with the closing of schools and places of business, parades, dancing in the streets, picnics, etc. But in Yisra'el the day of celebration is preceded by a day honoring and remembering those who gave their lives for the independence that we treasure.

Yom HaZikaron is a somber day that begins with a moment of silence for those who gave their lives in the War of Independence and in the battles that followed. No commercial television is aired, rather, appropriate programming highlighting the sacrifices made for independence are featured. Military cemeteries are crowded with family and friends paying their respects, as few families in Yisra'el are untouched by the decades of struggle to maintain the country's freedom. A second moment of silence at 11 am on *Yom Hazikaron* signals the beginning of special memorial ceremonies at the various cemeteries. The days ends with a ceremony on Mt. Herzl attended by State leaders, religious leaders and other dignitaries and viewed on television by the entire nation, and then the celebration of *Yom Ha'Asma'ut* begins.

This special anniversary is a time of reflection, seeing how far Yisra'el has come, and looking toward the future. The country's great achievements in so many diverse areas: agriculture, education, culture, and development, to name but a few. These are a great source of pride for Jews throughout the world.

Yom Yerushalayim

Yom Yerushalayim (Yerushalayim Day) – On June 7, 1967 Yisra'el i troops crashed through the defenses set up by Arab troops and recaptured those parts of the holy city of Yerushalayim that were previously in Arab possession. *Yom Yerushalayim* commemorates this significant day.

The Special Occasions
of Life

CHAPTER 16

Birth

The birth of a child into a Jewish home is one of the most joyous occasions in the life of a family. The Torah considers children a blessing from יהוה, bestowed on a family out of His kindness. Torah law surrounding birth is very brief:

> Male children must be circumcised (*see circumcision below*).

> Mothers after birth are *teme'ot* (impure) for a period of sixty days after the birth of a boy, and eighty days after the birth of a girl.

Birth Ceremonies

Karaites have two ceremonies that are associated with the birth of a child, one derived from the Torah, and one from traditional custom. *Berit Milah*, the circumcision of a male child, is prescribed by the Torah:

> Bere'shit 17.10
> This is the covenant that you and your descendants must keep: Each male among you must be circumcised;

221

The ceremony of *Berakhah LiQeri'yat Shem* [Naming Ceremony], was adopted to formally introduce a new girl child into the community.

Berit Milah

The *Berit Milah* occurs within the context of יהוה's renewed covenant promise to Avraham, following their initial contractual relationship (Bere'shit 15). While Avraham and his household were circumcised, יהוה 's command required that all Jewish male infants must be circumcised on the eighth day following their birth. This was distinctively different from contemporary pagan practices, which seem to have associated the rite either with puberty or with approaching marriage.

In the Torah, traditionally, the head of the family administered the *Milah*; however, the Torah records a special circumstance where a woman performed a *Milah* (Shemot 4.24-26). Today, a *Berit Milah* is usually performed by a mohel [ritual circumcisor].

Requirements For A *Berit Milah*

When a child is born (male or female), it is the responsibility of the father to let the *Bet Din* know of the birth as soon as possible.

The circumcision must take place on the 8th day following the child's birth (unless this will endanger its life). The 8th day is calculated by counting the day of birth as the first day, so that the weekday of circumcision will be the same as the weekday on which the child was born, one week later. Therefore, if a child was born on Wednesday, his *Milah* [circumcision] would be on the following Wednesday (Wayyiqra' 12.3).

During the ceremony, the *mohel* (ritual circumcisor) recites a special blessing over the child.

Customs Of The *Berit Milah*

Two days before the *Milah* is to take place, a special chair is sent to the home of the newborn (if this is where the *Milah* will take place), along with all the *mohel's* tools (if the *mohel* is of the community). The chair is a high-backed armchair with four poles extending out, upholstered in velvet and decorated with finials. The father or grandfather sits on this chair, holding the baby on his knees as the *mohel* performs the *Milah*.

Before the actual operation of circumcision takes place, the baby is gently tied with a satin sash to a special velvet *Berit* pillow, decorated with lace. The mother dons her wedding veil. The older sister of the baby, if she is of marriageable age, or any other older female relative (female is preferable), carries the baby, walking with the mother the father stands a short distance in front (she does not perform this because she is still *teme'ah* from the birth). The guests then sing and recite prayers as the mother, woman and baby walk back and forth seven times in front of the father. After this, another song is sung, the baby is handed to the father, and the *Milah* is performed.

Macaroons and almond pastries are traditional foods to serve at a *Berit Milah*.

It is customary to invite many people to attend a *Milah*; and it is generally, accompanied by a large feast.

Traditionally, a Karaite *Milah* involved the removal of the prepuce (the corona membrane is not uncovered, nor is the blood sucked out).

Naming Ceremony

The birth of a daughter is no less a blessing than the birth of a boy. Because there is no official ceremony in the Torah that inducts a girl in to the family of Yisra'el, we have adopted a naming ceremony that serves as a right of introduction for a baby girl into the community. The service for this ceremony can be found in Volume IV (*Berakhot*) of our *Siddur* [Prayer Book].

CHAPTER 17

Adoption and Conversion

Adoption

Children are at the center of the Jewish vision of family life. Today, more and more Jews are choosing to grow their families through adoption. Some couples adopt for altruistic reasons, often providing a home for older children or children with special needs. Some single Jews adopt because they want to raise a family and have been unsuccessful in finding a marriage partner. Nevertheless, most Jewish adoptions involve couples who are infertile and see adoption as the only alternative to building a family.

Experts estimate that 15% of all married couples have some kind of infertility problem, defined as being unsuccessful at achieving pregnancy after one year of trying. Among Jewish couples, the numbers may be even higher. The reason is that Jews tend to delay marriage and childbirth at a rate higher than the general population, with a subsequent lowering of fertility rates. While new reproductive medical techniques have helped many infertile couples,[1] yet for many couples, adoption is the only alternative.

Adoption is a wonderful way to build Jewish families; it provides homes for children whose birth parents cannot raise them and children for parents unable to achieve pregnancy. Nonetheless, adoption does raise numerous *halakhic* as well as practical questions for Jews.

In the *TaNaKh*, Avraham adopts his servant Eliezer and Mordehai raises his orphaned cousin Ester. According to the *TaNaKh* – Michal, the wife of King David – never birthed children all her life (Shemu'el Bet [2 Samuel] 6.23); however, the *TaNaKh* also mentions her five sons (Shemu'el Bet [2 Samuel] 21.8).

Adoption as practiced in our modern society means the removal of all rights and responsibilities of the biological parent, and their transfer to another couple or individual. For all intents and purposes, the child's biological lineage is broken. This procedure has its roots in ancient Roman law, where the concern was finding an heir for a childless couple. In contrast, British common law, coming from a society that placed great emphasis on lineage, bloodlines, and class, never developed an adoption procedure.

Jewish law is far closer to British common law, in this instance, than to ancient Roman law. In Judaism, personal status is based on bloodlines and lineage. The moment of birth gives a Jew his or her identity. No legal procedure or court decree can erase that.

This emphasis on bloodlines has serious consequences for adoption in Jewish law. For example, the status of the birth as Jew or gentile at the moment of birth establishes the identity of the child as Jewish or gentile (this is based on the lineage of the father).

The child is forbidden to marry certain paternal and maternal relatives, all based on their status at birth. No formal legal act can change this status. Based on this, any Jewish couple or single contemplating adoption should ascertain the status of the birthparents. If the child is Jewish, a couple will need to determine whether the child is a *Kohen, Levi,* or *Yisra'el.* Furthermore, it is important to have some documentation, preferably from the Karaite authority, as to the child's Jewish status. Such documentation can become vital, particularly if the child wishes to move to Yisra'el.

If a child is born of a gentile birth father, these issues do not arise. However, the child will need formal conversion to

Judaism (*see below*). This includes *Berit Milah* (if required), and purification. The conversion should be arranged at infancy, even though this is long before the child has understanding as to what is happening. However, at the age of understanding, when they are able to decide their religion for themselves, the child has the right either to reaffirm or to reject the conversion. That decision will ultimately determine their Jewish status.

Conversion

All individuals who are sincerely interested in converting to Karaite Judaism are welcome. No one who is serious is turned away. In the *TaNaKh* we can see from the book of Rut that even a Moabitess, normally forbidden, is acceptable as a convert if she is sincere. The 10th century *Hakham* Yefet Ben-'Eli HaLewi wrote in the introduction to his commentary on Rut that:

"Nobility of faith ranks higher than that of descent".

"We find also that he who is converted to the Jewish faith sometimes reaches a high position because of his obedience to יהוה".

"All this applies not only to men, but also to women".

"This is also true of the woman whose story we are about to explain, according to what is contained in the book bearing her name – meaning Ruth – wherein there is set for the excellence of her mind, conduct, and faith, because of which the Lord of the worlds joined her fate to that of that noble man, Bo'az, who was the ancestor of King David, so that Ruth became his wife. It will thus be shown that nobility of faith takes precedence over nobility of descent. Blessed therefore is he who dedicates himself to faith and makes it his strength and refuge, as it is written:

Psalms 2.12
Embrace purity lest you lose the way for His wrath is about to burn. Happy are all those that take refuge in [Him].'

Guidelines

There are some general guidelines for someone to follow in deciding whether or not they want to convert to Karaite Judaism:

Consider why you think being Jewish is important to you. Different people will have very different answers to these questions. Remember, Karaite Judaism is a religion, not a cultural affiliation.

Decide on the best time to approach the subject of conversion with your close friends and family. Your conversion will affect them significantly. In general, it is important to raise the subject as early as possible. Important moments in a family's history provide good times to discuss conversion.

If you find you are truly interested, the best first step is to have a talk with a *Hakham*, or knowledgeable Karaite. Some additional early activities include attending a Sabbath dinner and service – going to a Karaite Jewish ceremony, such as a wedding – taking an Introduction to Karaite Judaism class, reading about Karaite Judaism, etc.

IMPORTANT NOTE: Before attending a Karaite synagogue, one must ensure that they are ritually pure. For women, this entails that they should refrain from attending if they are having their period – and men should refrain if they find they have had a seminal (or other) emission. The best thing to do is contact a *Hakham* to discuss attendance, before coming to the synagogue.

Increasingly, there are people in the United States who are investigating Karaite Judaism. They did so because they found Judaism to be a wonderful way of life and because they found Jewish people who welcomed them.

Requirements For Conversion

The requirements for conversion to Karait Judaism are found in the Torah:

Shemot 12.48
"And when a stranger dwells with you [and wants] to keep the Passover to יהוה, let all his males be circumcised, and then let him come near and keep it; and he shall be as a native of the land. For no uncircumcised person shall eat it".

From this passage, and from inference, it is clear that a potential convert must do the following:

They must live in a Karaite community ("a stranger who dwells with you").

A man must be circumcised. If a family is converting, all males in that family must be circumcised ("let all his males be circumcised"). If a man, or all males in the family, are already circumcised, proof of this circumcision from a physician or other reputable source must be provided to the *Bet Din* certifying the conversion.

All converts must purify (make *tahor*) their homes and themselves.

A period of learning in the Karaite community, during which time the convert progressively beings to observe more and more of Jewish law, must elapse before the conversion can be certified. This usually takes between six months to a year.

Candidates for conversion must refrain from celebrating Passover until they have finalized their conversion (Shemot 12.48). This does not include the Festival of Unleavened Bread.

Upon finalizing their conversion, the convert makes a formal, legal, public declaration of their intent to convert and shun any other religions or religious systems.

CHAPTER 18

Marriage and Divorce

Marriage

The Jewish wedding ceremony is an intricate weaving of rituals, customs and liturgical elements. In the Torah the marriage is broken up into three different stages: Engagement, *mohar* (bride price and *ketubah* [marriage contract]), and Consummation. During the engagement phase, the couple are considered legally married, though they may not consummate their marriage until the bride price has been paid for by the groom. The terms of the *mohar* are detailed in the *ketubah* [marriage contract], which provides scope and definition to the arrangement being made between the family of the groom and bride. Consummation is the fulfillment of the engagement and *mohar*.

In Torah law, a marriage begins with engagement, and is considered legally binding at the point that the engagement is formally announced to the community. The formal announcement of engagement is considered a verbal contract. From the point of engagement, if the bride proves to be unfaithful, she is guilty of *ni'uf* ["adultery"]. Furthermore, there is a financial penalty that must be paid if the engagement is broken.

In the community, all engagements are recorded by the *Bet Din*. This includes the names of the bride and groom, family names, wedding date, responsibilities of each family, and the penalty to be paid if the engagement is broken.

Engagement Period Customs

Engagement parties, often held on *Purim*, are given to enable the members of both families to get to know each other.

At the engagement party, the bride and groom exchange gold rings with each other's names engraved on the inside of the ring. The bride wears the ring with her husband's name on it, and vice versa. The ring is accompanied by two things: a gift of jewelry, and a covered candy dish made of crystal silver or gold filled with *tahor* candy. It is presented by the groom to his bride wrapped in a white silk handkerchief with a sprig of rue. White signifies virginity, and the green of the rue good years in the future. If rue can not be found, myrtle is used.

The bride's trousseau customarily includes an Oriental rug, copper pots and pans, and a heavy brass mortar. Traditionally, as well, the trousseau is something a girl begins to make when she is in her teenage years.

One month before the wedding, invitations are sent out.

The dinner party before the wedding day is held at the home of the bride's family. The bride's family cooks and serves the meal.

A week before the wedding, the bride's trousseau is made public to the community at a trousseau party. Fried fish with hard rolls are customarily served at this gathering. On the following day, the trousseau is taken to the groom's house in a grand procession. The bride's family hires two or three open, horse drawn carriages with the trousseau inside to the accompaniment of a band. All the relatives wait at the groom's home for the caravan to arrive. The first item taken into the new home is a sprig of rue or myrtle.

Before the wedding takes place, the bride makes a *Tallit* and *Tallit* bag for her husband to be. These must be hand made, and she hand embroiders her husband's name on his *Tallit* bag.

The Wedding Ceremony

The wedding ceremony is very simple. The focus of the ceremony is the signing of the *ketubah* [marriage contract]. If there is no *Hazzan*, the ceremony is conducted entirely by the *Hakham*. The steps in the ceremony are as follows:

The *Hakham* asks the groom to take the vow that he is taking his wife with a *mohar* [bride price], *kitab* [marriage contract], and *bi'ah* [consummation]. The *Hakham* says the vow, and the groom repeats it word after word.

The groom then vows, in the same manner to take his wife in purity and holiness.

A passage from the book of Proverbs (Mishlei 3.4 – known as the *"Eshet Hayil"*) is read by the *Hakham* and attendees at the ceremony, antiphonally, reminding the groom of the importance of his wife, her family and her home.

The *ketubah* is then read aloud first in Hebrew, and then in the common language.

The *ketubah* is signed.

The *Hakham* repeats part of the *ketubah*, and has the groom and bride exchange rings.

A member of the family (bride or groom) places the *Tallit* made by the bride before the ceremony over the couple's heads, while the *Hakham* reads the blessing for the *Tallit*.

The *Hakham* asks יהוה to bless the bridge and groom, their home, and their new family with children, as he did with Peres.

Following this, seven blessings (*sheva berakhot*) are recited over the couple.

Once the *sheva berakhot* are complete, the *Hakham* asks the groom to drink from a cup of wine, while he asks יהוה to bless him and his house. This is repeated with the bride.

The *Tallit* is now lowered to the shoulders of the couple and the *Hakham* reminds them of the sad state of Yerushalayim. When he recites the words *Shuv meharon apekha*, the *Tallit* is raised over the couple's heads once again.

The ceremony is now complete; and the bride and groom are blessed again.

The *Hakham* asks the couple to kiss the Torah, which is placed on a table near the *Hakham*. When this is done, the guests start to sing *Amen Yehi Rason*.

Customs Of The Wedding Ceremony

Sundays and Tuesdays are reserved for the marriage of virgins being married for the first time.

Thursdays and Saturdays are reserved for women who were divorced or widowed.

The *ketubah* is signed and verified by ten witnesses at the *Bet Din.*

Intermarriage

Devarim 7.1-4

"When יהוה your God brings you into the land which you go to possess, and has cast out many nations before you, the Hittites and the Girgashites and the Amorites and the Cana'anites and the Perizzites and the Hivites and the Jebusites, seven nations greater and mightier than you, "and when יהוה your God delivers them over to you, you shall conquer them [and] utterly destroy them. You shall make no covenant with them nor show mercy to them. "Nor shall you make marriages with them. You shall not give your daughter to their son, nor take their daughter for your son. "For they will turn your sons away from following Me, to serve other gods; so the anger of יהוה will be aroused against you and destroy you suddenly..".

In Karaite law intermarriage refers not only to the marriage between a Jew and non-Jew, but to the marriage between a Karaite Jew and a Rabbanite Jew. Both types of unions are untenable, and should be avoided. This is, however, only in a case where the non-Karaite party is not interested in sincerely converting to Karaite Judaism.

We see very clearly that the *TaNaKh* approved of marriages between a Jew and non-Jew, assuming that the non-Jewish partner sincerely assumed the Jewish faith (cf. Rahab, and Ruth). The principle of not marrying unbelievers pervades the *TaNaKh* and appears to be the major concern of Ezra 9-10. He feared, in accordance with the Torah, that the daughters of foreign wives would lead men astray (as it did Solomon).

Divorce

> Devarim 24.1
> "When a man takes a wife and marries her, and it happens that she finds no favor in his eyes because he has found some uncleanness in her, and he writes her a certificate of divorce, puts [it] in her hand, and sends her out of his house..".

> Malachi 2.16
> "For יהוה God of Yisra'el says That He hates divorce, For it covers one's garment with violence", Says יהוה of hosts. "Therefore take heed to your spirit, That you do not deal treacherously".

While יהוה hates divorce, and it should be avoided at all costs, the Torah does allow for divorce when required (cf. Wayyiqra' 21.14; Deut 22.13-19, 28-29). In the Torah divorce is regulated in situations in which it might become common. It is not permitted: (1) when false accusations are made about a bride's virginity; and (2) when marriage occurred because a man had forcibly violated a woman sexually.[1] A priest cannot marry a divorcee. Devarim 24.1-4 prohibits remarriage of a woman to her first husband after the death or divorce of her second husband. The laws of the Torah surrounding divorce detail a legal policy whereby quick and frequent divorce is restrained and discouraged.

The basis for divorce, "some indecency" (*ervat dabar*), is found in Devarim 24.1, as above. The precise meaning of this phrase is uncertain. When the rest of the *TaNaKh* is examined, it appears that *ervat dabar* probably had sexual overtones—some lewd or immoral behavior including any sexual perversion, even adultery. The imagery of spiritual adultery, resulting in יהוה's "divorcing" Yisra'el (Isa 50.1; Jer 3.8), is based on a real referent. Divorce was socially permissible for adultery. Although adultery was punishable by death (Deut 22.22-24), it could still be included in the broad concept of *ervat dabar*. Whatever its true meaning, the text implies that *ervat dabar* was so vile that divorce was preferred by the husband. To protect the wife, however, he must provide her a certificate of divorce.

The Torah also recognizes and allows, without condemnation, the remarriage of the wife. In the time of the Torah remarriage would be expected since it was difficult for a woman to survive unless she was married or remained single in her father's house. It should be noted that the Torah prohibits remarriage to the first husband if the wife has taken another husband, as she has been known by another man.

Regulations Of Divorce

Either party may initiate divorce proceedings, however, the case for divorce must be brought to the *Bet Din*, where it will be evaluated.

If both parties agree to the divorce, it is granted immediately.

If the court determines that a woman's request for divorce is valid, even though the husband protests, the court will grant her divorce. The same situation applies to the husband.

Any ground for divorce caused by the person bringing the case for divorce is considered invalid.

The wife is entitled to three months of financial assistance during the waiting period after the divorce. If she is pregnant, the husband must take care of her through her delivery.

Appropriate grounds for divorce have been defined, but the list is quite long. What is important to remember is that divorce is not granted for any reason.

The *Bet Din* writes a document of divorce that is validated by both parties, and held by the wife. The bill of divorce may not specify the grounds for which the woman was divorced by her husband (if the husband initiates divorce).

A copy of the bill of divorce is held in the records of the *Bet Din*.

CHAPTER 19

Death and Mourning

Death

The Hebrew verb *gawa* which means "expire, breathe one's last", is used twenty-three times to describe death. Tehillim 104.29b says, "when you take away their breath, they die and return to the dust". "If it were his intention and he withdrew his spirit and breath, all mankind would perish" (Iyyov 34.14-15). Life and death are totally under יהוה's sovereignty. יהוה is the source of all life (Tehillim 36.9). There is nothing living that has not received its life from him: "In His hand is the life of every creature, and the breath of all mankind" (Job 12.10).

In the *TaNaKh*, death is more than the cessation of all physiological processes. By divine command (Tehillim 90.3), the body returns to dust and the spirit goes back to יהוה who gave it (Bere'shit 2.7; Qohelet 12.7).

The *TaNaKh* does hint at an afterlife, though it does not explicitly state that one exists. Deceased Shemu'el [Samuel] told Shaul [Saul] he and his sons would be with him the next day, implying that they would join him in death (Shemu'el Aleph [1 Samuel] 28.19). He could not have meant they would all be buried together the next day since Shaul's headless body was buried in Yabesh Gilad some time after his death (Shemu'el Aleph [1 Samuel] 31.9-11). Shemu'el [Samuel] was buried in his house at Ramah (Shemu'el Aleph [1 Samuel] 25.1); but in 28.13, 15, he comes up from the Earth to Shaul [Saul] at Endor protesting that he has been disturbed. The intense emotional

239

reaction of Shaul [Saul] and the medium, as well as their re-marks about Shemu'el [Samuel], indicate that they believed they had actually seen his departed spirit. Had this been some sort of delusion, the *TaNaKh* would certainly have mentioned this.

Death is an unavoidable reality. From a human point of view death is just as final as spilled water (Shemu'el Bet [2 Samuel] 14.14) and a pot broken at the well (Qohelet 12.6). Death is so ominous and powerful it can be compared to a fortified city with gates and bars (Tehillim 9.13; 107.18).

Our days are numbered (Bere'shit 6.3; Tehillim 90.10). They pass swiftly like the life of a flower (Tehillim 90.6; Isa 40.6). Thus the psalmist prays that we might number our days so as to live our lives carefully and wisely (Tehillim 90.12). Sometimes, the *TaNaKh* seems to respond rather pessimistically to death. The living know that they will die, but the dead do not know anything (Qohelet 9.5, 10). Men like Hezekiah could reason with יהוה that they should go on living because no one worships יהוה in death (Isa 28.18-19).

Qohelet even extols the advantages of death (Qohelet 4.2; cf. Job 3.13-19). He is not, however, as negative in his stance as is commonly supposed. Since death is quick and inevitable, mortals should live life intensely to the fullest, enjoying every minute of everything they do (Qohelet 9.10). יהוה has given them gifts of accepting their portion and finding satisfaction in their work (Qohelet 3.13; 5.17-18; 9.7). Since material things perish, we can best respond by orienting ourselves to the significant others יהוה has given us (Qohelet 9.9).

Fatalism is never a response to mortality. A live dog is better than a dead lion (Qohelet 9.4). Taking one's life is never recommended. Even in the Book of Iyyov it is never taken up as an option. The only victims of suicide in the *TaNaKh* were men (Ahithophel and Shaul [Saul]) who were faced with imminent, unavoidable death anyway. These men believed they were choosing a better manner of death than their enemies would select for them (Shemu'el Aleph [1 Samuel] 31.1-6; Shemu'el Bet [2 Samuel] 17.23).

Dealing With Mourning

We can find refuge in times of distress under the care of
יהוה (Tehillim 91.1). According to *Qohelet*, something about the
day of death is better than the day of birth (Qohelet 7.1).
Even though יהוה has set limits on human life, it is still valuable
and sacred to him. "Precious in the sight of יהוה is the death of his
righteous" (Tehillim 116.15). יהוה takes no pleasure even in the
death of the wicked (Yehezq'el 18.32).

For יהוה, death is not an insurmountable obstacle. The
death, indecision, barrenness, old age, and confusion of Bere'shit
11 actually becomes the stage on which יהוה begins to play out his
drama of redemption. Out of all this hopelessness and despair
comes the life-giving blessing of Bere'shit 12.1-3. Yesha'yahu
looks forward to a day when the death shroud will be removed,
and death will be permanently swallowed up (25.7-8).

Regulations And Customs Of Death And Mourning

The *Bet Din* should be informed of a death as soon
as possible so they can begin to make arrange-
ments for a funeral.

As soon as possible the members of the *Hebrat
Qaddisha* are sent to the residence of the deceased
to take care of the body.

Anyone who was present at the time of the death,
the room where the death occurred, and all open
vessels in the room (glasses, jars, vases) must be
purified on the first and seventh days following the
time of the death.

The funeral ceremony is conducted by a *Hakham*
or *Hazzan*.

After the funeral, there is a customary period of

mourning for thirty (30) days.

For the first seven days immediately following the funeral, one should take time off from work. Special prayer services are held each day, over the seven days.

During the course of the thirty (30) days of mourning, one should gradually work at returning to normal. Also, the tombstone should be cut during this time.

According to tradition, the period of mourning is defined by refraining from rejoicing of any kind: *bi'ah* (sexual intercourse), eating meat, listening to music, cutting hair, etc.

If *Hagh HaMassot* or *Sukkot* fall during the mourning period, the days of mourning are cut short in honor of the festival.

It is customary for mourners to sleep on the floor.

Everything in the house of a mourner is covered with black cloth.

CHAPTER 20

Teshuvah: Return

The most common term in the TaNaKh for repentance is shuv; the verbal forms appear well over 1,050 times. The most common translation for shuv is "turn" or "return". A related term is naham, which is often translated "repent".

The essence of repentance implied in shuv is to turn from evil,and turn to the good. Most critical, theologically, is the idea of returning to יהוה. Three times Yehezq'el included יהוה's call to the people of Yisra'el: "Turn! Turn from your idols and renounce all your detestable practices!" (Yehezq'el [Ezekiel] 14.6); "Turn! Turn away from all your offenses" (Yehezq'el [Ezekiel] 18.30); "Turn! Turn from your evil ways" (Yehezq'el [Ezekiel] 33.11). Such a call was characteristic of the prophets. The Septuagint underlines this idea by usually translating shuv by epi apo-strepho (to turn about, or to turn away from).

One may detect two sides to this turning. There is the free,sovereign act of יהוה's mercy, and a conscious decision to turn to יהוה (aturning that goes beyond sorrow and contrition).

Another aspect of *Teshuvah* is confession. Confession is both commanded and frequently illustrated (e.g., in the penitential prayers, as Tehillim [Psalms] 25 and 51). When one is guilty of various sins, "he must confess in what way he has sinned" in order to receive atonement and forgiveness (Wayyiqra' [Leviticus] 5.5; 26.40-42). In the Book of Yesha'yahu [Isaiah] 59.20 it states: "The Redeemer will come to Zion, to those in Jacob who turn from their sins".

The chief forms of repentance in the TaNaKh are cultic/ritual (e.g., expressed in public ceremonies, fasting, various displays of sorrow, liturgies, or days of repentance), and relational (e.g., the reparation of the covenantal relationship with יהוה).

יהוה wants very much for his children to return to them after they have turned away from Him. Amoz stated יהוה's lament that despite all He had done for or to the people, "yet you have not returned to me" (4.4, 8-11). Hoshe'a' anticipated the day when Yisra'el, "will return and seek יהוה their God and David their king" (Hoshe'a' 3.5). Thus he begged them to return to יהוה their God and to say, "Forgive all our sins and receive us graciously" (Hoshe'a' 14.2).

The use of the Hebrew word *naham* often refers to repenting. The basic sense is "being sorry, or grieved" for something that has been done. Frequently יהוה "relents" or "changes his dealings" with people. יהוה was "grieved" at human evil in the Earth, resulting in the flood (Bere'shit 6.6-7). He was "grieved" at having made Shaul king, and deposed him (Shemu'el Alef 15.11,26). Not infrequently יהוה relented and withheld predicted judgment on Yisra'el. An especially vivid illustration of this reversal is found in Hoshe'a' 11.8-9: "How can I give you up, Ephraim? ... My heart is changed within me... I will not carry out my fierce anger". This provides us with hope that יהוה's true love for Yisra'el will triumph through His covenant with us. Anyone who is truly repentant can return to יהוה, and His covenant.

Our Sages identified twelve points of full repentance, to serve as guidelines. They are:

> Aharon Ben-Eliyahu, Gan 'Eden
> There are twelve aspects to proper repentance. First, the true essence of repentance is regret of one's evil deeds. Second is the abandonment of the evil deed, Third is the hatred of it. Fourth is the submission to repentance with all its conditions. Fifth is confession. Sixth is the condition imposed by Torah as an accompaniment of repentance; while the Temple at Yerushalayim [Jerusalem] was standing, this was the duty to offer a sacrifice, but

now there remains on the utterance of our lips, as it is written: "so will we render for bulls the offering of our lips","(Hosheah 14.3). Seventh, man must not postpone repentance for long after the feeling of regret – like the one who says, "I will sin now and repent later" – unless he is compelled by circumstances beyond his control to do so. Eight, he must renounce the evil deed for the sake of its very vileness. Ninth, he must also not do anything like it in the future. Tenth, he must take it upon himself not to do it again at another time. Eleventh, he must do repentance with the intention of canceling the punishment for his evil deed. Twelfth, he must do repentance because it is a duty...

Appendix

Karaite Contributions

Karaites have made several important contributions to Judaism and the world. This section details some of those contributions.

Aharon Ben-Mosheh Ben-Asher

Aharon Ben-Mosheh Ben-Asher lived in Tiberius during the first half of the 10th century. His family had been involved in creating and maintaining the *Masorah* (the preservation of the Torah) for either five or six generations. Ben-Asher rapidly gained fame as the most authoritative of the Tiberias Masoretes, and, even after his death, his name continued to hold respect.

In 989 C.E. an unknown scribe of a Former Prophets manuscript vouched for the care with which his copy was written by claiming that he had vocalized and added the *Masorah* "from the books that were [vocalized] by Aharon Ben-Mosheh Ben-Asher".

Mosheh Ben-Maimon (called the RaMBaM), by accepting the views of Ben-Asher, helped establish and spread his authority. Referring to a Bible manuscript then in Egypt, he wrote: "All relied on it, since it was corrected by Ben-Asher and was worked on and analyzed by him for many years, and was proofread many times in accordance with the *Masorah*, and I based myself on this manuscript in the *Sefer* Torah that I wrote".

Since most Torah scribes today continue to rely on the writing rules of RaMBaM as their guide, the Masorah as established by Aharon Ben-Mosheh Ben-Asher was influential indeed. His vocalization of the Bible is still used by all Jews to this day.

Significantly, Aharon Ben-Mosheh Ben-Asher was the first to take Hebrew grammar seriously. He was the first systematic Hebrew grammarian. His *Sefer Dikdukei ha-Te'amim*

(Grammar of the Vocalizations) was an original collection of grammatical rules and Masoretic information. Grammatical principles were not at that time considered worthy of independent study. The value of this work is that the grammatical rules presented by Ben-Asher reveal the linguistic background of vocalization for the first time. He had a tremendous influence on the world of Biblical grammar and scholarship.

Ya'aqov Al-Qirqisani

Besides his work as a legal authority, Ya'aqov al-Qiriqsani was, as well, a world-class historian; and modern historians are deeply in his debt. One of the most important, and widely translated of his works, is the first section of his *Kitabu 'l-Anwar wa-'l-Maraqib*, which details the Jewish sects that were prevalent in his day (and some which had preceded it). A master academician, Qirisani also preserved volumes of information on modern science and thought. Aside from what information there is in his works, little is known about Qirqisani's life.

Yishaq Troki

As his name indicates, Yishaq Troki was born in Troki. Receiving a thorough Karaite and secular education, Troki spoke Latin and Polish and held conversations on theological subjects with Catholic, Protestant and Greek Orthodox clergymen. Using the material he gleaned from his conversations, he wrote his famous apology of Judaism, *Hizzuk Emmunah* (the strengthening of faith), which has become the classic Jewish refutation of the Christian faith. Its penetrating examination of the vulnerable points of Christianity caused it to be translated into Latin with an extensive refutation, under the name *"Tela ignea Satanæ"* (the fiery darts of Satan). Voltaire used some of its arguments and mentioned it as a masterpiece of its kind. Troki might have been dismayed at its notoriety, - he had intended it for use by Jewish scholars only. *Hizzuk Emmunah* remains a classic work that is widely consulted in Jewish circles to this day.

Colophon:

This volume was the product of the efforts of several people – both directly, and indirectly – among them are: Yosef el-Gamil, Hayyim Levi, Avraham Qanaï, Yosef Yaron, and Joe Pesah. An Introduction to Karaite Judaism was based on an idea from Joe Pesah. It was compiled by Yosef Yaron, and edited by Avraham Qanaï, Yosef Yaron, Ana Yaron, Joe Pessah and Henry Mourad. Most translations were provided by Avraham Qanaï. This project was funded by the al-Qirqisani Center for the Promotion of Karaite Studies. Thanks are also extended to Dr. Phillip Miller and Dr. Daniel Frank who gave graciously of their time to review sections of this volume.

Index